Rise: Mastering Confidence, Mindfulness, And Self-Esteem

Travis Breeding

Published by Travis Breeding, 2024.

While every precaution has been taken in the preparation of this book, the publisher assumes no responsibility for errors or omissions, or for damages resulting from the use of the information contained herein.

RISE: MASTERING CONFIDENCE, MINDFULNESS, AND SELF-ESTEEM

First edition. February 21, 2024.

Copyright © 2024 Travis Breeding.

ISBN: 979-8223544043

Written by Travis Breeding.

Also by Travis Breeding

Harmony in Flux: Navigating Bi-Polar Brilliance
The Friendship Rainbow
The Great Kindergarten Adventure: A Story about Going to School with Autism
The Magic Forest Adventure
Unlocking Brilliance: Navigating Autism and Applied Behavior Analysis Towards a Radiant Future
Decoding Love: Navigating Dating and Relationships on the Autism Spectrum
Echoes of a Late Diagnosis: Unveiling the Spectrum Within
From Theory to Practice: Implementing Effective Autism Interventions St
The Amazing Adventures of Aiden and His Asperger's Superpowers
The Magical Adventures of Lily and the Enchanted Forest
Unlocking Potential: A Journey Of Discovery Through ABA Therapy
Unlocking Potential: Navigating Employment for Neurodiverse Talent
Unlocking the Spectrum: A Journey through Applied Behavior Analysis from an Autistic Perspective
Unlocking The Spectrum: Navigating The Complexity Of Autism With Advanced Strategies And Insights
Beyond The Spectrum: Insights From Autistic Adults
Beyond The Stereotypes
Breaking Barriers: Navigating Autism With Therapeutic Insight
Celebrating Neurodiversity

Embracing Differences
From Diagnosis To Treatment
From Dreams To Reality: The Young President
Living With Autism: A Journey Of Triumph And Challenges
Neurodiversity Unveiled: Navigating The Spectrum Of Inclusion
Sunshine At Disney World
The Art Of Reinforcement
The Magical School Bus Ride: A Journey Of Understanding
ThroughThe Spectrum Of Love
Dancing With Shadows: How To Turn Your Fears Into Powerful
Allies
From Chaos To Control: How To Develop Strong Executive
functioning Skills
From Misunderstood To Mainstream
Unlocking the Spectrum: A Comprehensive Guide to Understanding
and Thriving with Autism
Unraveling The Mind: Understanding OCD, Autism, And Obsession
Rise: Mastering Confidence, Mindfulness, And Self-Esteem

Watch for more at breedingautismconsulting.com.

Table of Contents

Chapter 1: From Small Beginnings to Great Success: The Journey of Growth

Growth is a fundamental aspect of personal and professional development. It is the process of continuous improvement and learning that allows individuals to reach their full potential. Whether it is in our careers, relationships, or personal lives, growth plays a crucial role in shaping who we are and what we can achieve.

The benefits of continuous growth are numerous. It allows us to expand our knowledge and skills, adapt to new situations, and overcome challenges. It also helps us build resilience, confidence, and a sense of purpose. By constantly seeking growth, we can unlock new opportunities, achieve our goals, and lead fulfilling lives.

The Importance of Starting Small

Starting small is often the key to achieving long-term success. It allows us to build a solid foundation and gain valuable experience along the way. Many successful individuals started with humble beginnings and gradually worked their way up.

For example, Oprah Winfrey began her career as a local news anchor before eventually becoming one of the most influential media moguls in the world. Jeff Bezos started Amazon as an online bookstore before expanding it into the e-commerce giant it is today. These individuals understood the importance of starting small and taking incremental steps towards their goals.

Starting small also helps us develop important skills such as patience, perseverance, and resourcefulness. It allows us to learn from our mistakes and make necessary adjustments along the way. By starting small, we can build momentum and gradually work towards bigger goals.

The Role of Persistence in Achieving Success

Persistence is a crucial trait for achieving success. It is the ability to keep going despite obstacles, setbacks, and failures. Without persistence, it is easy to give up when faced with challenges.

Many successful individuals have demonstrated persistence in their journeys towards success. Thomas Edison failed thousands of times before finally inventing the light bulb. J.K. Rowling faced numerous rejections before finding a publisher for her Harry Potter series. These individuals understood that persistence is often the key to overcoming obstacles and achieving their goals.

Persistence is not just about pushing through difficult times, but also about learning from failures and making necessary adjustments. It requires a growth mindset and the willingness to adapt and try new approaches. By persisting in the face of challenges, we can develop resilience and achieve our desired outcomes.

Overcoming Challenges on the Path to Growth

On the path to growth, individuals often face various challenges that can hinder their progress. These challenges can include fear of failure, self-doubt, lack of resources, and external obstacles. However, with the right strategies, these challenges can be overcome.

One common challenge is the fear of failure. Many individuals are afraid to take risks or try new things because they fear they will fail.

However, failure is an essential part of the growth process. It provides valuable lessons and insights that can lead to future success. By reframing failure as a learning opportunity, individuals can overcome their fear and embrace growth.

Another challenge is self-doubt. Many individuals doubt their abilities and question whether they are capable of achieving their goals. However, self-doubt is often unfounded and can be overcome through self-belief and positive affirmations. By focusing on our strengths and accomplishments, we can build confidence and overcome self-doubt.

Lack of resources can also be a challenge on the path to growth. However, resourcefulness is a valuable skill that can help individuals overcome this challenge. By thinking creatively and finding alternative solutions, individuals can make the most of the resources they have and continue to grow.

The Benefits of Learning from Failure

Failure is often seen as something negative, but it is an important part of the growth process. It provides valuable feedback and insights that can lead to future success. Many successful individuals have learned from their failures and used them as stepping stones towards achieving their goals.

For example, Steve Jobs was famously fired from Apple, the company he co-founded. However, he used this setback as an opportunity to start a new company, NeXT, which eventually led to his return to Apple and the creation of iconic products like the iPhone and iPad. Jobs understood that failure is not the end, but rather a chance to learn and grow.

By embracing failure and learning from it, individuals can develop resilience, adaptability, and problem-solving skills. It also helps individuals develop a growth mindset, which is the belief that abilities can be developed through dedication and hard work. By viewing failure as a temporary setback rather than a reflection of their abilities, individuals can continue to grow and achieve their goals.

The Impact of Mindset on Growth

Mindset plays a crucial role in personal and professional growth. A growth mindset is the belief that abilities can be developed through dedication and hard work. It is the belief that intelligence and talent are not fixed traits, but rather qualities that can be cultivated over time.

Having a growth mindset is important because it allows individuals to embrace challenges, persist in the face of obstacles, and learn from failures. It helps individuals view setbacks as opportunities for growth rather than as indicators of their abilities. By adopting a growth mindset, individuals can unlock their full potential and achieve their goals.

There are several strategies for developing a growth mindset. One strategy is to reframe challenges as opportunities for growth. Instead of viewing challenges as something to be avoided or feared, individuals with a growth mindset see them as chances to learn and improve.

Another strategy is to focus on effort rather than outcomes. Individuals with a growth mindset understand that effort is what leads to growth and improvement. By focusing on effort rather than outcomes, individuals can develop a love for learning and a willingness to take on new challenges.

The Value of Setting Goals and Tracking Progress

Setting goals and tracking progress is important for growth because it provides direction and motivation. Goals give individuals something to strive for and help them stay focused on their desired outcomes. By setting clear and specific goals, individuals can create a roadmap for their growth.

Tracking progress is also important because it allows individuals to see how far they have come and identify areas for improvement. It provides a sense of accomplishment and helps individuals stay motivated. By tracking progress, individuals can make necessary adjustments and continue to grow.

When setting goals, it is important to make them specific, measurable, achievable, relevant, and time-bound (SMART). Specific goals are clear and well-defined. Measurable goals can be tracked and evaluated. Achievable goals are realistic and attainable. Relevant goals align with an individual's values and aspirations. Time-bound goals have a deadline or timeframe.

The Role of Networking and Collaboration in Growth

Networking and collaboration play a crucial role in achieving growth. Building a strong network allows individuals to connect with like-minded individuals, learn from others' experiences, and gain new perspectives. It also provides access to opportunities, resources, and support.

Networking can be done both online and offline. Online networking platforms such as LinkedIn allow individuals to connect with professionals in their field and join relevant groups or communities. Offline networking can be done through attending industry events, conferences, or workshops.

Collaboration is also important for growth because it allows individuals to leverage the strengths and expertise of others. By collaborating with others, individuals can learn new skills, gain different perspectives, and achieve more than they could on their own. Collaboration can take many forms, such as partnering on a project, joining a mastermind group, or seeking mentorship.

When building a network or collaborating with others, it is important to be genuine, supportive, and willing to give as much as you receive. Building strong relationships takes time and effort but can lead to long-term growth and success.

The Importance of Adaptability and Flexibility

Adaptability and flexibility are important qualities for growth because they allow individuals to navigate change and uncertainty. In today's fast-paced and ever-changing world, the ability to adapt and embrace new opportunities is crucial.

Adaptability is the ability to adjust to new situations, challenges, or environments. It requires individuals to be open-minded, willing to learn, and able to think creatively. By being adaptable, individuals can seize new opportunities, overcome obstacles, and continue to grow.

Flexibility is the ability to change course or adjust plans when necessary. It requires individuals to be open to feedback, willing to make adjustments, and able to let go of rigid thinking. By being flexible, individuals can respond to changing circumstances and make necessary changes to achieve their goals.

Developing adaptability and flexibility can be done through exposure to new experiences, seeking feedback from others, and embracing change. It is also important to cultivate a growth mindset and view challenges as opportunities for growth rather than as obstacles.

The Rewards of Embracing Change and Innovation

Embracing change and innovation is crucial for growth because it allows individuals to stay ahead of the curve and seize new opportunities. Change is inevitable in today's rapidly evolving world, and those who resist it often get left behind.

Embracing change requires individuals to be open-minded, curious, and willing to learn. It also requires a willingness to take risks and try new approaches. By embracing change, individuals can adapt to new technologies, trends, and ways of doing things.

Innovation is the process of creating something new or improving existing products, services, or processes. It requires individuals to think creatively, challenge the status quo, and take calculated risks. By embracing innovation, individuals can find new solutions to problems, create value for others, and achieve growth.

Many successful individuals and companies have embraced change and innovation to achieve success. For example, Apple revolutionized the music industry with the introduction of the iPod and iTunes. Netflix disrupted the traditional video rental industry by introducing a streaming service. These individuals and companies understood the importance of embracing change and innovation to stay relevant and achieve growth.

Embracing the Journey of Growth

In conclusion, growth is a powerful force that can transform our lives and help us reach our full potential. By starting small, persisting in the face of challenges, learning from failure, developing a growth mindset, setting goals, building a strong network, being adaptable, and embracing change and innovation, we can continue to grow and achieve personal and professional success.

The journey of growth is not always easy, but it is worth it. It requires dedication, hard work, and a willingness to step outside of our comfort zones. However, the rewards are immense. By embracing the journey of growth, we can unlock new opportunities, overcome obstacles, and lead fulfilling lives.

So, let us embrace the power of growth and continue to pursue personal and professional development. Let us start small, persist in the face of challenges, learn from failure, develop a growth mindset, set goals, build a strong network, be adaptable, and embrace change and innovation. By doing so, we can create a life filled with purpose, success, and continuous growth.

Chapter 2: Unleashing Your Inner Power: A Guide to Empowerment

Inner power refers to the strength and potential that lies within each individual. It is the ability to tap into our inner resources, beliefs, and strengths to overcome challenges, achieve success, and live a fulfilling life. This concept recognizes that we have the power to shape our own lives and make positive changes.

Tapping into our inner power is crucial because it allows us to take control of our lives and make choices that align with our values and goals. It empowers us to overcome obstacles, face adversity, and achieve personal growth. By understanding and harnessing our inner power, we can unlock our full potential and create a life that is meaningful and fulfilling.

In this blog post, we will explore various aspects of inner power and provide practical strategies for tapping into it. We will discuss how to identify our strengths, overcome limiting beliefs, set goals, take action, build resilience, embrace change, cultivate self-compassion, connect with others, practice mindfulness and meditation, and ultimately unlock our inner power for a fulfilling life.

Identifying Your Strengths: Uncovering Your Inner Power

One of the first steps in tapping into your inner power is identifying your strengths. Self-reflection exercises can help you uncover your unique abilities, talents, and qualities that make you who you are. By recognizing and acknowledging your strengths, you can empower yourself to use them to your advantage.

Start by asking yourself questions such as: What am I good at? What do I enjoy doing? What comes naturally to me? What do others appreciate about me? Reflect on your past experiences and achievements to identify patterns or themes that highlight your strengths.

Once you have identified your strengths, find ways to use them in different areas of your life. For example, if you are good at problem-solving, you can apply this strength in your work or personal life by taking on challenging projects or helping others find solutions to their problems. By leveraging your strengths, you can boost your confidence, increase your effectiveness, and ultimately empower yourself to achieve your goals.

There are many examples of people who have harnessed their inner power through identifying their strengths. Take Oprah Winfrey, for instance. She recognized her ability to connect with people and communicate effectively, which led her to become one of the most influential media personalities in the world. By embracing her strengths and using them to make a positive impact, she has empowered herself and inspired millions of others.

Overcoming Limiting Beliefs: Breaking Free from Negative Self-Talk

Limiting beliefs are negative thoughts or beliefs that hold us back from reaching our full potential. They often stem from past experiences, societal conditioning, or self-doubt. Overcoming these limiting beliefs is essential for tapping into our inner power and living a fulfilling life.

Common limiting beliefs include thoughts such as "I'm not good enough," "I don't deserve success," or "I will never be able to achieve my goals." These beliefs create self-doubt and prevent us from taking risks or pursuing our dreams.

To overcome limiting beliefs, it is important to challenge them and replace them with more empowering thoughts. Start by identifying the specific limiting beliefs that are holding you back. Write them down and examine the evidence for and against each belief. Often, you will find that there is little or no evidence to support these beliefs.

Next, reframe these limiting beliefs into more positive and empowering statements. For example, instead of saying "I'm not good enough," you can reframe it as "I am capable of learning and growing." Repeat these positive affirmations regularly to reprogram your subconscious mind and reinforce empowering beliefs.

The power of positive affirmations cannot be underestimated. By consistently repeating positive statements about yourself and your abilities, you can rewire your brain and change your mindset. Over time, these affirmations will become ingrained in your subconscious mind, boosting your confidence and empowering you to overcome challenges.

Setting Goals: Harnessing Your Inner Power to Achieve Success

Setting goals is a powerful way to tap into your inner power and achieve success. Goals provide direction, motivation, and a sense of purpose. They give you something to strive for and help you stay focused on what is important to you.

When setting goals, it is important to make them specific, measurable, achievable, relevant, and time-bound (SMART). This ensures that your goals are clear, realistic, and within your control. Break down your goals into smaller, manageable steps to make them more attainable.

To stay motivated and focused on your goals, it can be helpful to visualize your success. Imagine yourself achieving your goals and experiencing the positive emotions associated with it. This visualization technique can help you stay motivated and remind you of the rewards that await you.

Additionally, it is important to regularly review and reassess your goals. As you progress towards your goals, you may need to make adjustments or set new goals. This flexibility allows you to adapt to changing circumstances and continue moving forward.

By setting goals and harnessing your inner power, you can create a roadmap for success and empower yourself to take the necessary actions to achieve your dreams.

Taking Action: Empowering Yourself through Proactivity

Taking action is a crucial step in tapping into your inner power. It is not enough to simply set goals; you must also take consistent action towards them. Action is what transforms dreams into reality.

Procrastination is one of the biggest obstacles to taking action. It is easy to get caught up in distractions or fear of failure. To overcome procrastination, break tasks down into smaller, manageable steps. This makes them less overwhelming and more achievable.

Another strategy for overcoming procrastination is to create a schedule or routine that includes dedicated time for working towards your goals. By making your goals a priority and allocating specific time for them, you are more likely to follow through and take action.

Accountability is also important in taking consistent action. Find ways to hold yourself accountable, such as sharing your goals with a trusted friend or family member, joining a support group, or hiring a coach or mentor. These external sources of accountability can help you stay on track and motivated.

Remember that taking imperfect action is better than not taking any action at all. Embrace the idea of progress over perfection and be willing to learn from your mistakes. Each step you take towards your goals is a step closer to unlocking your inner power and achieving success.

Building Resilience: Strengthening Your Inner Power in the Face of Adversity

Resilience is the ability to bounce back from setbacks, adapt to change, and thrive in the face of adversity. It is an essential aspect of tapping into your inner power and living a fulfilling life.

Building resilience involves developing coping mechanisms, cultivating a positive mindset, and learning from challenges. One strategy for building resilience is to reframe setbacks as opportunities for growth. Instead of viewing failures as personal shortcomings, see them as valuable learning experiences that can help you become stronger and more resilient.

Another strategy for building resilience is to practice self-care. Take care of your physical, mental, and emotional well-being by getting enough sleep, eating nutritious food, exercising regularly, and engaging in activities that bring you joy and relaxation. When you prioritize self-care, you are better equipped to handle stress and adversity.

Seeking support from others is also important in building resilience. Surround yourself with positive and supportive people who can provide encouragement, guidance, and perspective. Sharing your challenges with others can help you gain new insights and find solutions to problems.

There are many examples of people who have overcome adversity through resilience. One such example is J.K. Rowling, the author of the Harry Potter series. She faced numerous rejections before finding success, but she persevered and used her setbacks as fuel for her creativity. Her resilience and determination ultimately led to the creation of one of the most beloved book series of all time.

Embracing Change: Using Your Inner Power to Adapt and Thrive

Change is inevitable in life, and embracing it is essential for tapping into your inner power. Change can be uncomfortable and challenging, but it also presents opportunities for growth and transformation.

To embrace change, it is important to adopt a growth mindset. This means viewing challenges as opportunities for learning and personal development. Instead of resisting change, approach it with curiosity and openness. Ask yourself what you can learn from the situation and how you can use it to your advantage.

Another strategy for embracing change is to focus on what you can control. While there may be aspects of a situation that are beyond your control, you always have the power to choose how you respond to it. By focusing on what you can control, you can empower yourself to take proactive steps towards positive change.

Using change as an opportunity for growth and empowerment requires flexibility and adaptability. Be willing to let go of old ways of thinking or doing things that no longer serve you. Embrace new ideas, perspectives, and approaches. By embracing change, you can tap into your inner power and create a life that is aligned with your values and goals.

Cultivating Self-Compassion: Nurturing Your Inner Power with Kindness

Self-compassion is the practice of treating yourself with kindness, understanding, and acceptance, especially in times of difficulty or failure. It is an essential aspect of tapping into your inner power and living a fulfilling life.

Cultivating self-compassion involves being kind to yourself, acknowledging your imperfections, and recognizing that everyone makes mistakes. Instead of beating yourself up over failures or setbacks, offer yourself the same kindness and understanding that you would offer to a friend.

One strategy for cultivating self-compassion is to practice self-care. Take time to engage in activities that bring you joy, relaxation, and rejuvenation. Prioritize your physical, mental, and emotional well-being.

Another strategy for cultivating self-compassion is to challenge your inner critic. Notice when negative self-talk arises and replace it with more compassionate and supportive thoughts. Remind yourself that you are human and that making mistakes is a natural part of the learning process.

Self-compassion can empower you to overcome challenges by providing a sense of safety and support. It allows you to approach difficulties with a mindset of growth and resilience, rather than self-judgment or criticism. By nurturing your inner power with kindness, you can tap into your full potential and create a life that is filled with self-acceptance and fulfillment.

Connecting with Others: Empowering Yourself and Others through Positive Relationships

Positive relationships have the power to empower us and tap into our inner power. When we surround ourselves with supportive and uplifting people, we are more likely to feel motivated, inspired, and empowered.

Building positive relationships involves being intentional about the people we choose to spend our time with. Seek out individuals who share similar values, goals, and interests. Surround yourself with people who believe in you, encourage you, and challenge you to grow.

Strategies for building positive relationships include active listening, empathy, and open communication. Show genuine interest in others by listening attentively and asking thoughtful questions. Practice empathy by putting yourself in their shoes and trying to understand their perspective. Communicate openly and honestly, expressing your needs, boundaries, and feelings.

Positive relationships can empower us by providing emotional support, guidance, accountability, and inspiration. They can also serve as a source of motivation and encouragement during challenging times. By connecting with others and building positive relationships, you can tap into your inner power and create a support system that helps you thrive.

Mindfulness and Meditation: Tapping into Your Inner Power through Awareness

Mindfulness and meditation are powerful practices that can help us tap into our inner power and live a more fulfilling life. They involve cultivating awareness of the present moment, without judgment or attachment.

The benefits of mindfulness and meditation are numerous. They can reduce stress, improve focus and concentration, enhance self-awareness, increase emotional resilience, and promote overall well-being. By practicing mindfulness and meditation, we can tap into our inner wisdom, intuition, and creativity.

To incorporate mindfulness into your daily routine, start by setting aside a few minutes each day for quiet reflection. Find a comfortable space where you can sit or lie down without distractions. Close your eyes and focus on your breath, observing the sensations as you inhale and exhale. Whenever your mind wanders, gently bring your attention back to your breath.

Meditation involves focusing your attention on a specific object, such as your breath, a mantra, or a visualization. Find a meditation technique that resonates with you and practice it regularly. Start with short sessions and gradually increase the duration as you become more comfortable.

By incorporating mindfulness and meditation into your daily routine, you can tap into your inner power and live a more present, peaceful, and fulfilling life.

Unlocking Your Inner Power for a Fulfilling Life

In conclusion, tapping into your inner power is essential for living a fulfilling life. By identifying your strengths, overcoming limiting beliefs, setting goals, taking action, building resilience, embracing change, cultivating self-compassion, connecting with others, practicing mindfulness and meditation, you can unlock your full potential and create a life that is aligned with your values and goals.

Remember that unlocking your inner power is an ongoing process. It requires self-reflection, self-awareness, and a commitment to personal growth. Be patient with yourself and celebrate your progress along the way.

By tapping into your inner power, you can overcome challenges, achieve success, and live a life that is meaningful and fulfilling. You have the power within you to create the life you desire. Embrace your inner power and unlock your full potential.

Chapter 3: The Power of Resilience: How to Bounce Back from Life's Challenges

Resilience is the ability to bounce back from adversity, to adapt and recover quickly from difficult situations. It is the capacity to withstand and overcome challenges, setbacks, and stressors in life. Resilience is not about avoiding or denying difficult experiences, but rather about facing them head-on and finding ways to navigate through them. It is an essential skill that can help individuals thrive in the face of adversity.

Resilience is important because life is full of ups and downs. We all face challenges, setbacks, and stressors at some point in our lives. Whether it's a personal loss, a job loss, a health issue, or a global pandemic, resilience allows us to cope with these challenges and come out stronger on the other side. It helps us maintain a positive outlook, adapt to change, and find solutions to problems. Resilience is not only important for our mental and emotional well-being but also for our physical health and overall life satisfaction.

Understanding the Science of Resilience: How it Works in the Brain and Body

The brain plays a crucial role in resilience. It is responsible for processing information, regulating emotions, and making decisions. When faced with a stressful situation, the brain activates the body's stress response system, releasing hormones like cortisol and adrenaline. These hormones prepare the body for fight or flight, increasing heart rate, blood pressure, and alertness.

However, chronic stress can have detrimental effects on the body. It can lead to physical health problems like high blood pressure, heart disease, and weakened immune system. It can also impact mental health, leading to anxiety disorders, depression, and burnout.

Resilience can help mitigate the effects of stress on the body. Research has shown that resilient individuals have lower levels of stress hormones and better immune function compared to those who are less resilient. They are better able to regulate their emotions and maintain a positive outlook, even in the face of adversity. Resilience also helps individuals develop effective coping strategies and problem-solving skills, allowing them to navigate through difficult situations more effectively.

The Benefits of Resilience: How it Can Improve Your Life

Resilience has numerous benefits that can improve various aspects of our lives. Firstly, it improves mental health. Resilient individuals are better able to cope with stress, anxiety, and depression. They have a positive outlook on life and are more likely to seek help when needed. Resilience also helps individuals develop strong social connections and support networks, which are crucial for mental well-being.

Secondly, resilience improves physical health. Chronic stress can have a negative impact on the body, leading to various health problems. Resilient individuals are better able to manage stress and maintain a healthy lifestyle. They engage in regular exercise, eat a balanced diet, and get enough sleep, all of which contribute to better physical health.

Lastly, resilience increases happiness and life satisfaction. When faced with challenges, resilient individuals are able to find meaning and purpose in their experiences. They see setbacks as opportunities for growth and learning. They have a sense of control over their lives and are more likely to set goals and work towards them. This sense of purpose and accomplishment leads to increased happiness and overall life satisfaction.

The Characteristics of Resilient People: What Sets Them Apart

Resilient people possess certain characteristics that set them apart from others. Firstly, they have a positive attitude. They believe in their ability to overcome challenges and view setbacks as temporary obstacles rather than permanent failures. They maintain a hopeful outlook even in difficult times.

Secondly, resilient people are adaptable. They are able to adjust their thoughts, behaviors, and emotions in response to changing circumstances. They are open-minded and willing to try new approaches when faced with challenges. They see change as an opportunity for growth and development.

Lastly, resilient people have strong problem-solving skills. They are able to identify the root causes of problems and come up with effective solutions. They are resourceful and creative in finding ways to overcome obstacles. They are not afraid to ask for help when needed and are willing to learn from their mistakes.

Overcoming Adversity: How to Build Resilience in the Face of Challenges

Building resilience is a lifelong process that requires effort and practice. Here are some strategies to help build resilience in the face of challenges:

1. Accepting change: Change is inevitable in life, and accepting it is the first step towards building resilience. Embrace the idea that change can lead to growth and new opportunities.

2. Learning from failure: Failure is a natural part of life, and resilient individuals see it as a learning experience rather than a reflection of their worth. Reflect on your failures, identify what went wrong, and use that knowledge to improve and grow.

3. Seeking support: Building a strong support network is crucial for resilience. Surround yourself with positive and supportive people who can provide emotional support, guidance, and encouragement during difficult times.

Developing a Resilient Mindset: How to Cultivate a Positive Attitude

Developing a resilient mindset is essential for building resilience. Here are some strategies to cultivate a positive attitude:

1. Practicing gratitude: Take time each day to reflect on the things you are grateful for. This helps shift your focus from negative to positive aspects of your life.

2. Focusing on strengths: Identify your strengths and use them to overcome challenges. Focus on what you can do rather than what you can't.

3. Developing a growth mindset: Embrace the belief that you can learn and grow from every experience. See setbacks as opportunities for growth and improvement.

Coping Strategies for Resilience: How to Manage Stress and Anxiety

Managing stress and anxiety is crucial for building resilience. Here are some coping strategies that can help:

1. Mindfulness meditation: Practice mindfulness meditation to help calm the mind and reduce stress. Focus on the present moment and let go of worries about the past or future.

2. Exercise: Engage in regular physical activity to release endorphins, which are natural mood boosters. Exercise also helps reduce stress and improve overall well-being.

3. Journaling: Write down your thoughts and feelings in a journal. This can help you gain clarity, process emotions, and find solutions to problems.

Building Resilience in Children: How to Help Kids Bounce Back from Life's Challenges

Building resilience in children is important for their overall well-being and future success. Here are some strategies to help kids bounce back from life's challenges:

1. Encouraging independence: Allow children to take on age-appropriate responsibilities and make decisions for themselves. This helps build their confidence and problem-solving skills.

2. Teaching problem-solving skills: Teach children how to identify problems, brainstorm solutions, and evaluate the effectiveness of different approaches. Encourage them to think critically and creatively.

3. Providing emotional support: Be there for your child emotionally, providing a safe and supportive environment where they can express their feelings and seek guidance when needed.

Resilience in the Workplace: How to Build a Resilient Team

Building a resilient team is crucial for success in the workplace. Here are some strategies to build resilience in the workplace:

1. Encouraging open communication: Foster an environment where team members feel comfortable expressing their thoughts, concerns, and ideas. Encourage open dialogue and active listening.

2. Providing opportunities for growth and development: Offer training programs, workshops, and mentorship opportunities to help employees develop new skills and grow professionally.

3. Fostering a positive work environment: Create a positive and supportive work culture where employees feel valued, appreciated, and motivated. Recognize and reward their efforts and achievements.

The Role of Support Systems in Resilience: How to Build a Strong Network

Building a strong support network is crucial for resilience. Here are some strategies to build a strong network:

1. Building relationships with family and friends: Cultivate meaningful relationships with family and friends who provide emotional support, guidance, and encouragement.

2. Seeking out professional support: If needed, seek out professional support from therapists, counselors, or coaches who can provide guidance and help develop coping strategies.

3. Joining a community or group: Join communities or groups that share similar interests or experiences. This can provide a sense of belonging and support during difficult times.

How Resilience Can Help You Thrive in Life

In conclusion, resilience is an essential skill that can help individuals thrive in life. It allows us to bounce back from adversity, adapt to change, and find solutions to problems. Resilience improves mental and physical health, increases happiness and life satisfaction, and helps us navigate through life's challenges more effectively.

Building resilience requires effort and practice. It involves developing a positive attitude, cultivating a resilient mindset, and using coping strategies to manage stress and anxiety. Building resilience in children, in the workplace, and within support systems is also important for overall well-being and success.

By building resilience in everyday life, we can face challenges with confidence, maintain a positive outlook, and thrive in the face of adversity.

Chapter 4: Mindfulness for Beginners: A Step-by-Step Guide to Finding Inner Peace

Mindfulness is the practice of intentionally paying attention to the present moment without judgment. It involves bringing awareness to our thoughts, feelings, bodily sensations, and the surrounding environment. In today's fast-paced and often stressful world, mindfulness has become increasingly important in helping individuals find balance and peace in their daily lives.

The importance of mindfulness in daily life cannot be overstated. It allows us to cultivate a greater sense of self-awareness and helps us to better understand our thoughts and emotions. By practicing mindfulness, we can learn to respond to situations rather than react impulsively, leading to more thoughtful and intentional actions. Additionally, mindfulness has been shown to have numerous benefits for mental health, including reducing stress and anxiety, improving focus and concentration, enhancing emotional regulation, and boosting overall well-being.

Understanding the Benefits of Mindfulness for Mental Health

A. Reducing stress and anxiety

One of the most well-known benefits of mindfulness is its ability to reduce stress and anxiety. When we practice mindfulness, we are able to bring our attention to the present moment, rather than getting caught up in worries about the future or regrets about the past. This can help to calm the mind and reduce feelings of stress and anxiety.

B. Improving focus and concentration

In today's digital age, it can be challenging to stay focused on one task at a time. However, practicing mindfulness can help improve our ability to concentrate and stay focused. By training our minds to stay present in the moment, we can become more attentive and engaged in whatever we are doing.

C. Enhancing emotional regulation

Mindfulness can also help us regulate our emotions more effectively. By bringing awareness to our emotions as they arise, we can learn to observe them without judgment or attachment. This allows us to respond to our emotions in a more skillful way, rather than reacting impulsively or getting overwhelmed by them.

D. Boosting overall well-being

In addition to its mental health benefits, mindfulness has also been shown to have a positive impact on overall well-being. Research has found that regular mindfulness practice can lead to increased feelings of happiness, contentment, and overall life satisfaction. It can also improve physical health by reducing blood pressure, improving sleep quality, and boosting the immune system.

The Science Behind Mindfulness and How It Affects the Brain

A. Explanation of the brain's default mode network

The brain's default mode network is a network of brain regions that are active when we are not focused on the outside world. It is responsible for mind-wandering, self-referential thinking, and daydreaming. When we practice mindfulness, we activate a different network in the brain known as the task-positive network, which is associated with attention and focus.

B. How mindfulness affects the brain's structure and function

Research has shown that regular mindfulness practice can lead to changes in the structure and function of the brain. For example, studies have found that mindfulness can increase the thickness of the prefrontal cortex, which is involved in executive functions such as decision-making and self-control. It can also decrease the size of the amygdala, which is responsible for processing emotions.

C. The role of neuroplasticity in mindfulness

Neuroplasticity refers to the brain's ability to change and adapt throughout our lives. Mindfulness has been found to promote neuroplasticity by strengthening existing neural connections and creating new ones. This means that with regular practice, we can actually rewire our brains to become more mindful and resilient.

How to Prepare for a Mindfulness Practice

A. Setting up a comfortable space

Before starting a mindfulness practice, it's important to create a comfortable space where you can relax and focus without distractions. This could be a quiet room in your home or even just a corner of your bedroom. Make sure the space is clean and clutter-free, and consider adding elements that promote relaxation, such as candles or soft lighting.

B. Choosing a time of day

Finding a time of day that works best for you is crucial in establishing a regular mindfulness practice. Some people prefer to practice in the morning to start their day off on a calm and centered note, while others find it helpful to practice in the evening to unwind and let go of the day's stress. Experiment with different times and see what works best for you.

C. Selecting a mindfulness technique

There are many different mindfulness techniques to choose from, so it's important to find one that resonates with you. Some popular techniques include breath awareness, body scan meditation, loving-kindness meditation, and walking meditation. Try out different techniques and see which one feels most natural and enjoyable for you.

Step-by-Step Guide to Mindfulness Meditation for Beginners

A. Finding a comfortable seated position

To begin your mindfulness meditation practice, find a comfortable seated position. You can sit on a cushion or chair with your back straight but not rigid. Rest your hands on your lap or thighs, and close your eyes or lower your gaze.

B. Focusing on the breath

Once you are settled in your seated position, bring your attention to your breath. Notice the sensation of the breath as it enters and leaves your body. You can focus on the rising and falling of your abdomen or the feeling of air passing through your nostrils.

C. Acknowledging distractions without judgment

As you focus on your breath, you may notice thoughts, emotions, or physical sensations arising in your awareness. Instead of getting caught up in these distractions, simply acknowledge them without judgment and gently bring your attention back to the breath.

D. Returning to the breath

Throughout your meditation practice, you will likely find that your mind wanders away from the breath multiple times. This is completely normal and to be expected. Each time you notice your mind has wandered, simply bring your attention back to the breath, without judgment or frustration.

Tips for Staying Focused During Mindfulness Meditation

A. Using guided meditations

If you find it challenging to stay focused during mindfulness meditation, using guided meditations can be helpful. Guided meditations provide verbal instructions and prompts to help keep your attention on the present moment. There are many apps and websites that offer free guided meditations for beginners.

B. Incorporating mindfulness into daily routines

Another way to stay focused during mindfulness meditation is to incorporate mindfulness into your daily routines. For example, you can practice mindful eating by paying attention to the taste, texture, and smell of your food. You can also practice mindful walking by bringing awareness to the sensations in your feet as they touch the ground.

C. Practicing self-compassion

It's important to remember that mindfulness is a practice, and it's natural for the mind to wander and for distractions to arise. Instead of getting frustrated or judging yourself for not being "good" at mindfulness, practice self-compassion. Treat yourself with kindness and understanding, and gently bring your attention back to the present moment whenever you notice it has wandered.

Incorporating Mindfulness into Daily Life: Practical Strategies

A. Mindful eating

Mindful eating involves bringing awareness to the experience of eating, including the taste, texture, and smell of food. To practice mindful eating, try to eat without distractions, such as TV or your phone. Take small bites and chew slowly, savoring each bite. Notice how the food makes you feel physically and emotionally.

B. Mindful communication

Mindful communication involves being fully present and attentive when interacting with others. Instead of thinking about what you're going to say next or getting caught up in judgments or assumptions, listen to the other person with an open mind and heart. Notice your own reactions and emotions as they arise, and respond with kindness and understanding.

C. Mindful movement

Mindful movement practices, such as yoga or tai chi, can help bring awareness to the body and cultivate a sense of presence. When practicing mindful movement, focus on the sensations in your body as you move, paying attention to your breath and the physical sensations of stretching and moving.

Mindful Breathing Exercises for Stress Relief

A. Deep breathing

Deep breathing is a simple yet effective mindfulness technique that can help reduce stress and promote relaxation. To practice deep breathing, sit or lie down in a comfortable position. Take a slow, deep breath in through your nose, allowing your belly to rise. Then exhale slowly through your mouth, letting go of any tension or stress.

B. Counting breaths

Counting breaths is another mindfulness technique that can help calm the mind and bring focus to the present moment. To practice counting breaths, simply count each inhale and exhale, starting from one and going up to ten. If you lose count or get distracted, simply start over from one.

C. Alternate nostril breathing

Alternate nostril breathing is a more advanced breathing technique that can help balance the energy in the body and calm the mind. To practice alternate nostril breathing, sit in a comfortable position and use your right thumb to close your right nostril. Inhale deeply through your left nostril, then use your right ring finger to close your left nostril as you exhale through your right nostril. Continue alternating sides for several rounds.

Mindful Movement: Yoga and Other Physical Practices

A. Explanation of yoga and its benefits

Yoga is a mindful movement practice that combines physical postures, breath control, and meditation. It has been practiced for thousands of years and has numerous benefits for both the body and mind. Yoga can improve flexibility, strength, and balance, as well as reduce stress and promote relaxation.

B. Other mindful movement practices

In addition to yoga, there are many other mindful movement practices that can help cultivate presence and awareness. These include tai chi, qigong, Pilates, and dance. Each of these practices involves moving the body with intention and focus, bringing awareness to the sensations in the body as you move.

C. How to incorporate mindful movement into daily life

To incorporate mindful movement into your daily life, try to find opportunities to move with awareness and presence. This could be as simple as taking a mindful walk in nature, practicing yoga or tai chi in the morning, or even just stretching and moving your body mindfully throughout the day. The key is to bring your attention to the physical sensations in your body as you move, rather than getting caught up in thoughts or distractions.

Overcoming Common Challenges in Mindfulness Practice

A. Dealing with distractions

Distractions are a common challenge in mindfulness practice, but they can be overcome with patience and practice. When distractions arise, simply acknowledge them without judgment and gently bring your attention back to the present moment. It can also be helpful to label distractions as "thinking" or "feeling" to create some distance from them.

B. Managing discomfort

Physical discomfort is another common challenge in mindfulness practice, especially when sitting for long periods of time. If you experience discomfort, try adjusting your posture or using props such as cushions or blankets for support. You can also experiment with different seated positions or try practicing mindfulness lying down or while walking.

C. Staying motivated

Staying motivated to maintain a regular mindfulness practice can be challenging, especially when life gets busy or stressful. To stay motivated, remind yourself of the benefits of mindfulness and how it has positively impacted your life. Set realistic goals and create a routine that works for you. It can also be helpful to find a community or support system, such as a meditation group or online forum, to stay connected and inspired.

The Long-Term Benefits of a Regular Mindfulness Practice

A. Improved mental and physical health

Regular mindfulness practice has been shown to have numerous long-term benefits for mental and physical health. It can reduce symptoms of anxiety and depression, improve sleep quality, lower blood pressure, and boost the immune system. It can also increase resilience and help individuals better cope with stress and adversity.

B. Increased self-awareness

Mindfulness practice cultivates self-awareness by bringing attention to our thoughts, emotions, and bodily sensations. Over time, this increased self-awareness can lead to a deeper understanding of ourselves and our patterns of behavior. It can also help us recognize and break free from unhelpful habits or thought patterns.

C. Enhanced relationships

Mindfulness can also have a positive impact on our relationships with others. By practicing mindfulness, we become more present and attentive when interacting with others, which can improve communication and deepen connections. Mindfulness also helps us cultivate qualities such as compassion, empathy, and non-judgment, which are essential for healthy relationships.

D. Greater sense of purpose and meaning

Finally, regular mindfulness practice can lead to a greater sense of purpose and meaning in life. By bringing awareness to the present moment, we can fully engage in our experiences and find joy in the simple things. Mindfulness also helps us connect with our values and priorities, allowing us to live a more authentic and fulfilling life.

In conclusion, mindfulness is a powerful practice that has numerous benefits for mental health and overall well-being. By bringing awareness to the present moment without judgment, we can reduce stress and anxiety, improve focus and concentration, enhance emotional regulation, and boost overall happiness and life satisfaction. The science behind mindfulness shows that it can actually change the structure and function of the brain, promoting neuroplasticity and resilience. By incorporating mindfulness into our daily lives through practices such as meditation, mindful eating, and mindful movement, we can experience the long-term benefits of improved mental and physical health, increased self-awareness, enhanced relationships, and a greater sense of purpose and meaning. So why not start a mindfulness practice today and begin reaping the many benefits it has to offer?

Chapter 5: Unleashing Your Inner Confidence: Tips and Tricks for a More Empowered You

Self-confidence is a crucial aspect of our lives that can greatly impact our overall well-being and success. It is the belief in oneself and one's abilities, which allows individuals to face challenges, take risks, and pursue their goals with determination. Self-confidence is not only important for personal growth but also for professional success and healthy relationships. In this article, we will explore the importance of self-confidence and provide practical tips on how to boost it.

Understanding the Importance of Self-Confidence

Self-confidence can be defined as a belief in one's own abilities and worth. It is the foundation upon which we build our lives and pursue our dreams. Having self-confidence allows us to overcome obstacles, take risks, and bounce back from failures. It gives us the courage to step out of our comfort zones and embrace new opportunities.

The benefits of having self-confidence are numerous. Firstly, it enhances our overall well-being by reducing stress and anxiety. When we believe in ourselves, we are less likely to worry about what others think or fear failure. This leads to increased happiness and a more positive outlook on life.

Self-confidence also plays a crucial role in our professional lives. It allows us to showcase our skills and talents, take on leadership roles, and pursue career advancement opportunities. Employers are more likely to trust and promote individuals who exude confidence in their abilities.

In relationships, self-confidence is equally important. It enables us to communicate effectively, set boundaries, and maintain healthy connections with others. When we believe in ourselves, we are more likely to attract positive relationships and avoid toxic ones.

Recognizing Your Strengths and Weaknesses

Self-awareness is a key component of self-confidence. It involves recognizing and understanding our strengths and weaknesses. By identifying our strengths, we can leverage them to achieve success and build confidence. On the other hand, acknowledging our weaknesses allows us to work on improving them and develop a growth mindset.

To recognize your strengths, reflect on your past achievements and moments when you felt proud of yourself. Consider the skills and qualities that helped you succeed in those situations. These strengths can be anything from being a good listener to having strong problem-solving abilities.

Identifying weaknesses can be more challenging as it requires honest self-reflection. Ask yourself what areas you struggle with or where you feel less confident. It could be public speaking, time management, or assertiveness. Once you have identified your weaknesses, make a plan to improve them. This could involve seeking additional training or seeking guidance from a mentor.

Setting Realistic Goals to Boost Confidence

Setting goals is an effective way to boost self-confidence. When we set goals and achieve them, we prove to ourselves that we are capable of success. However, it is important to set realistic goals that are attainable and aligned with our abilities and resources.

To set realistic goals, start by defining what you want to achieve. Be specific about what you want and why it is important to you. Break down your goal into smaller, manageable steps that you can take towards achieving it. This will make the goal less overwhelming and increase your chances of success.

It is also important to set deadlines for each step and hold yourself accountable. This will help you stay focused and motivated. Celebrate each milestone along the way to boost your confidence and keep yourself motivated.

Overcoming Self-Doubt and Negative Thoughts

Self-doubt and negative thoughts can be major obstacles to self-confidence. They can hold us back from pursuing our goals and undermine our belief in ourselves. However, it is possible to overcome these negative thoughts and replace them with positive ones.

Common negative thoughts include "I'm not good enough," "I will fail," or "I don't deserve success." To overcome these thoughts, challenge them with evidence of your past successes and achievements. Remind yourself of times when you have overcome challenges and achieved your goals. Surround yourself with positive affirmations and quotes that inspire and motivate you.

Techniques for managing self-doubt include practicing mindfulness and self-compassion. Mindfulness involves being present in the moment and observing your thoughts without judgment. This can help you detach from negative thoughts and focus on the present moment. Self-compassion involves treating yourself with kindness and understanding, just as you would treat a friend. Be gentle with yourself and remind yourself that everyone makes mistakes and faces challenges.

Embracing Your Unique Qualities

Embracing your unique qualities is essential for building self-confidence. Each of us has a unique set of skills, talents, and qualities that make us who we are. By embracing these qualities, we can develop a sense of self-worth and confidence.

To embrace your unique qualities, start by identifying what makes you special. Reflect on your strengths, passions, and values. Consider what sets you apart from others and what makes you unique. Embrace these qualities and use them to your advantage in pursuing your goals.

It is also important to surround yourself with people who appreciate and value your uniqueness. Seek out supportive friends, mentors, or communities that celebrate diversity and individuality. Surrounding yourself with positive influences will boost your confidence and help you embrace your unique qualities.

Practicing Positive Self-Talk

Positive self-talk is a powerful tool for building self-confidence. It involves replacing negative thoughts with positive ones and speaking to yourself in a kind and encouraging manner. By practicing positive self-talk, you can rewire your brain to focus on your strengths and achievements.

To practice positive self-talk, start by becoming aware of your inner dialogue. Notice when negative thoughts arise and challenge them with positive affirmations. For example, if you catch yourself thinking "I can't do this," replace it with "I am capable and have overcome challenges before."

Another technique for practicing positive self-talk is to create a list of positive affirmations. These are statements that reflect your strengths, abilities, and goals. Repeat these affirmations to yourself daily, especially in moments of self-doubt or before facing a challenging situation.

Stepping Out of Your Comfort Zone

Stepping out of your comfort zone is essential for building self-confidence. It involves taking risks, facing fears, and embracing new experiences. When we step out of our comfort zones, we prove to ourselves that we are capable of growth and success.

To step out of your comfort zone, start by identifying areas where you feel stuck or limited. This could be trying a new hobby, speaking up in meetings, or taking on a leadership role. Start small and gradually increase the level of challenge as you become more comfortable.

It is important to remember that stepping out of your comfort zone does not mean throwing yourself into the deep end. Take calculated risks and set realistic goals for yourself. Celebrate each step outside your comfort zone, regardless of the outcome, as it is a sign of growth and progress.

Dressing for Success: How Your Appearance Affects Confidence

Your appearance can have a significant impact on your confidence levels. When you dress well and feel good about your appearance, you are more likely to exude confidence and make a positive impression on others.

Dressing for success involves wearing clothes that make you feel comfortable, confident, and aligned with your personal style. Choose outfits that flatter your body shape and highlight your best features. Pay attention to grooming and personal hygiene to ensure you feel polished and put together.

It is also important to dress appropriately for different occasions. Consider the dress code and expectations of the environment you will be in. Dressing appropriately shows respect for yourself and others and can boost your confidence in social or professional settings.

Building a Support System

Building a support system is crucial for maintaining and boosting self-confidence. Surrounding yourself with positive, supportive individuals can provide encouragement, guidance, and a sense of belonging.

To build a support system, start by identifying individuals who uplift and inspire you. These could be friends, family members, mentors, or colleagues. Reach out to them and express your desire to build a supportive network. Attend networking events or join communities that align with your interests and goals.

It is important to nurture these relationships by being supportive and offering help when needed. Celebrate each other's successes and provide encouragement during challenging times. A strong support system can provide a safe space to share your fears and insecurities and receive valuable feedback and advice.

Taking Care of Your Mental and Physical Health

Taking care of your mental and physical health is essential for building self-confidence. When we prioritize our well-being, we feel more energized, focused, and capable of achieving our goals.

To take care of your mental health, practice self-care activities that bring you joy and relaxation. This could include exercise, meditation, journaling, or spending time in nature. Prioritize activities that help you unwind and recharge.

Taking care of your physical health involves eating a balanced diet, getting regular exercise, and getting enough sleep. These habits not only improve your physical well-being but also boost your mood and energy levels. When you feel physically healthy, you are more likely to feel confident in your abilities.

Celebrating Your Achievements and Progress

Celebrating your achievements and progress is crucial for building self-confidence. It allows you to acknowledge your hard work and success, no matter how small. By celebrating your achievements, you reinforce positive behaviors and boost your confidence for future endeavors.

To celebrate your achievements, set aside time to reflect on your progress regularly. Keep a journal or create a vision board to track your goals and milestones. When you achieve a goal or make progress towards it, reward yourself with something meaningful to you. This could be treating yourself to a spa day, going on a weekend getaway, or simply taking time to relax and enjoy your accomplishment.

It is important to remember that celebrating your achievements does not mean comparing yourself to others. Focus on your own journey and progress and avoid the trap of comparison. Each achievement, no matter how small, is a step towards building self-confidence and achieving your goals.

Self-confidence is a crucial aspect of our lives that impacts our overall well-being, success, and relationships. By recognizing our strengths and weaknesses, setting realistic goals, overcoming self-doubt, embracing our unique qualities, practicing positive self-talk, stepping out of our comfort zones, dressing for success, building a support system, taking care of our mental and physical health, and celebrating our achievements and progress, we can boost our self-confidence and live fulfilling lives. Implementing these tips requires commitment and practice but the rewards are well worth it. So go ahead, believe in yourself and take the necessary steps to build your self-confidence. You deserve it!

Chapter 6: The Power of Visualization in Goal-Setting: How to Manifest Your Desires

Visualization is a powerful tool that can help individuals achieve their goals and manifest their desires. It involves creating a mental image or picture of what you want to achieve, and then focusing on that image with intention and belief. By visualizing your goals, you are able to tap into the power of your subconscious mind and align your thoughts, beliefs, and actions with your desired outcome.

Visualization is not just a new age concept; it has been used by successful individuals throughout history. Athletes, entrepreneurs, and artists have all utilized visualization techniques to enhance their performance and achieve their goals. By visualizing success, you are able to create a clear vision of what you want to achieve, which in turn helps you stay focused and motivated.

The Science Behind Visualization: How it Affects Your Brain and Your Reality

The power of visualization lies in its ability to affect both the brain and the body. When you visualize a goal or desire, your brain actually interprets it as a real experience. This activates the same neural pathways and releases the same neurotransmitters as if you were actually experiencing the event in real life. This means that by visualizing success, you are training your brain to believe that it is possible, which in turn increases your motivation and confidence.

Furthermore, visualization is closely connected to the law of attraction. The law of attraction states that like attracts like, meaning that by focusing on positive thoughts and emotions, you attract positive experiences into your life. When you visualize your goals with positive emotions such as joy, gratitude, and excitement, you are sending out a powerful signal to the universe that you are ready to receive what you desire. This helps to align your energy with your goals and attract the opportunities and resources needed to achieve them.

Setting Your Goals: Defining Your Desires and Creating a Clear Vision

Before you can effectively visualize your goals, it is important to first define what you truly desire. Setting clear and specific goals is essential for successful visualization. Take the time to reflect on what you truly want in life, whether it is in your personal or professional life. Write down your goals and be as specific as possible. For example, instead of saying "I want to be successful," specify what success means to you and what it looks like.

Once you have defined your desires, it is important to create a clear vision of what you want to achieve. This involves creating a mental image of your desired outcome and focusing on the details. Imagine yourself already achieving your goal and immerse yourself in the experience. What does it feel like? What do you see, hear, and smell? The more vivid and detailed your visualization, the more powerful it will be.

The Art of Visualization: Techniques to Help You Visualize Your Goals

There are several different techniques that can help enhance your visualization practice. One technique is guided visualization, where you listen to a recording or follow along with a script that guides you through a visualization exercise. This can be especially helpful for beginners who may find it difficult to create their own visualizations.

Another technique is creative visualization, where you use your imagination to create a mental image of your desired outcome. This can be done by closing your eyes and imagining yourself already achieving your goal. Visualize the details and immerse yourself in the experience. You can also use props or symbols to enhance your visualization, such as holding an object that represents your goal or creating a vision board.

Creating a Vision Board: How to Use Visual Aids to Manifest Your Desires

A vision board is a powerful tool that can help you manifest your desires by creating a visual representation of your goals and dreams. It is essentially a collage of images, words, and symbols that represent what you want to achieve. By creating a vision board, you are able to bring your goals to life and keep them at the forefront of your mind.

To create a vision board, start by gathering magazines, newspapers, or printouts of images that resonate with your goals. Cut out the images and words that represent what you want to achieve and arrange them on a poster board or corkboard. You can also add personal photos or drawings to make it more meaningful. Place your vision board in a location where you will see it every day, such as your bedroom or office, and spend a few minutes each day visualizing your goals as you look at the images.

The Power of Affirmations: How Positive Self-Talk Can Help You
Achieve Your Goals

Affirmations are positive statements that you repeat to yourself to
reinforce positive beliefs and thoughts. They can be a powerful tool for
enhancing your visualization practice and aligning your subconscious
mind with your goals. By repeating affirmations, you are able to
reprogram your subconscious mind and replace negative beliefs with
positive ones.

To create effective affirmations, start by identifying any negative
beliefs or self-doubt that may be holding you back. Then, create
positive statements that counteract these negative beliefs. For example,
if you have a belief that you are not good enough, you can create an
affirmation such as "I am worthy of success and abundance." Repeat
these affirmations daily, preferably in front of a mirror, and truly believe
in the words you are saying.

Overcoming Obstacles: Using Visualization to Overcome Challenges
and Limiting Beliefs

Visualization can be a powerful tool for overcoming obstacles and
limiting beliefs that may be holding you back from achieving your
goals. By visualizing yourself successfully overcoming challenges, you
are able to build confidence and belief in your abilities. This helps to
rewire your brain and replace negative thoughts with positive ones.

When faced with a challenge or obstacle, take a few moments to
visualize yourself successfully overcoming it. Imagine yourself finding
a solution, staying calm and focused, and achieving your desired
outcome. By visualizing success, you are able to tap into your inner

resources and find the motivation and confidence needed to overcome any obstacle.

The Role of Emotions: How to Harness the Power of Your Emotions to Manifest Your Desires

Emotions play a crucial role in the visualization process. When you visualize your goals with positive emotions such as joy, gratitude, and excitement, you are able to amplify the power of your visualizations. This is because emotions are a powerful energy that can help attract what you desire into your life.

To harness the power of your emotions, it is important to cultivate positive emotions on a daily basis. Practice gratitude by focusing on the things you are grateful for in your life. Find activities that bring you joy and make you feel alive. Surround yourself with positive people who uplift and inspire you. By cultivating positive emotions, you are able to enhance your visualization practice and attract more positive experiences into your life.

The Importance of Consistency: How to Stay Committed to Your Visualization Practice

Consistency is key when it comes to visualization. It is important to make visualization a daily practice in order to see results. Just like any other skill, the more you practice, the better you become. Set aside a specific time each day to visualize your goals, whether it is in the morning or before bed. Make it a non-negotiable part of your routine.

To stay committed to your visualization practice, it can be helpful to create a ritual or routine around it. Find a quiet and comfortable space where you can relax and focus on your visualizations. You can also incorporate other practices such as meditation or journaling to enhance your visualization practice. The key is to make it a priority and treat it as an important part of your personal and professional growth.

Celebrating Your Success: How to Acknowledge Your Achievements and Keep Moving Forward

Celebrating your successes is an important part of the visualization process. By acknowledging and celebrating your achievements, you are able to stay motivated and inspired to keep moving forward. Take the time to reflect on your progress and give yourself credit for the steps you have taken towards your goals.

One way to celebrate your successes is to keep a gratitude journal. Write down your achievements, big or small, and express gratitude for them. You can also reward yourself with something meaningful whenever you achieve a milestone or reach a goal. This can be as simple as treating yourself to a nice meal or taking a day off to relax and recharge. The key is to acknowledge your achievements and give yourself the recognition you deserve.

Embracing the Power of Visualization to Create the Life You Desire

In conclusion, visualization is a powerful tool that can help individuals achieve their goals and manifest their desires. By creating a clear vision of what you want to achieve and visualizing it with intention and belief, you are able to tap into the power of your subconscious mind and align your thoughts, beliefs, and actions with your desired outcome.

The science behind visualization shows that it affects both the brain and the body, activating neural pathways and releasing neurotransmitters that increase motivation and confidence. Visualization is closely connected to the law of attraction, as it helps align your energy with your goals and attract the opportunities and resources needed to achieve them.

By setting clear goals, using visualization techniques, creating a vision board, practicing affirmations, overcoming obstacles, harnessing the power of emotions, staying consistent, and celebrating your successes, you can embrace the power of visualization and create the life you desire. Visualization is not just a new age concept; it is a proven technique used by successful individuals throughout history. So why not give it a try? Start visualizing your goals today and watch as your dreams become a reality.

Chapter 7: Discovering Your True Self: The Journey to Self-Awareness

Self-awareness is the ability to introspect and recognize one's own thoughts, emotions, and behaviors. It involves being conscious of oneself and having a clear understanding of one's strengths, weaknesses, values, beliefs, and motivations. Self-awareness is a crucial aspect of personal growth and development as it allows individuals to make informed decisions, build healthy relationships, and live an authentic life.

Self-awareness is the foundation of personal growth and development. It provides individuals with the opportunity to understand themselves on a deeper level and make conscious choices that align with their true selves. By being self-aware, individuals can identify their strengths and weaknesses, allowing them to focus on areas for improvement and personal growth. It also enables individuals to recognize their values, beliefs, and motivations, which are essential in guiding their actions and decisions.

Why is Discovering Your True Self Important?

Discovering your true self is important because it allows you to live an authentic life. When you are in touch with your true self, you are able to align your actions and decisions with your values and beliefs. This authenticity leads to a sense of fulfillment and satisfaction in life. Living authentically also allows you to build genuine connections with others, as they are able to see and appreciate the real you.

Understanding your values, beliefs, and motivations is crucial in making informed decisions. When you are aware of what truly matters to you, you can make choices that align with your core principles. This leads to a sense of purpose and direction in life. By making decisions that are in line with your true self, you are more likely to experience success and fulfillment.

Building healthy relationships is another important aspect of discovering your true self. When you are aware of who you are and what you want in life, you are better equipped to form meaningful connections with others. You can establish boundaries that protect your well-being and engage in relationships that are mutually beneficial. By being true to yourself, you attract people who appreciate and respect you for who you are.

The Benefits of Self-Awareness: A Closer Look

Self-awareness has numerous benefits that contribute to personal growth and development. One of the key benefits is improved emotional intelligence. When you are self-aware, you are able to recognize and understand your own emotions, as well as the emotions of others. This allows you to navigate social situations with empathy and understanding, leading to stronger relationships and effective communication.

Another benefit of self-awareness is better decision-making skills. When you have a clear understanding of your values, beliefs, and motivations, you can make decisions that align with your true self. This leads to more confident and informed choices, resulting in positive outcomes. Self-awareness also helps individuals recognize their biases and blind spots, allowing them to make more objective decisions.

Increased self-confidence is another advantage of self-awareness. When you have a deep understanding of yourself, including your strengths and weaknesses, you can approach challenges with confidence. Self-awareness allows individuals to recognize their abilities and leverage them effectively, leading to increased self-esteem and belief in one's own capabilities.

Greater empathy and understanding of others is also a benefit of self-awareness. When individuals are aware of their own thoughts, emotions, and behaviors, they are better able to relate to the experiences of others. This leads to more compassionate and empathetic interactions, fostering stronger relationships and a sense of connection with others.

The Obstacles to Self-Awareness: Overcoming Self-Doubt and Fear

While self-awareness is crucial for personal growth and development, there are often obstacles that can hinder the process. One common barrier is self-doubt. Many individuals struggle with negative self-talk and a lack of confidence in their abilities. This can prevent them from truly understanding themselves and embracing their true selves. Overcoming self-doubt requires challenging negative beliefs and replacing them with positive affirmations. It also involves seeking support from others and practicing self-compassion.

Fear is another obstacle to self-awareness. Fear of judgment, failure, or rejection can prevent individuals from exploring their true selves and taking risks. Overcoming fear involves stepping out of one's comfort zone and embracing vulnerability. It requires individuals to confront their fears head-on and take small steps towards personal growth. By facing fear, individuals can discover their true selves and unlock their full potential.

The Power of Reflection: How to Look Inward and Discover Your True Self

Self-reflection is a powerful tool for self-awareness. It involves taking the time to look inward and examine one's thoughts, emotions, and behaviors. Self-reflection allows individuals to gain insight into their own experiences and understand themselves on a deeper level.

There are several techniques that can be used for self-reflection. Journaling is a popular method that involves writing down one's thoughts and feelings. This allows individuals to process their experiences and gain clarity about their emotions and motivations. Meditation is another effective technique for self-reflection. By practicing mindfulness and focusing on the present moment, individuals can gain insight into their thoughts and emotions.

Mindfulness and Meditation: Techniques for Cultivating Self-Awareness

Mindfulness is the practice of being fully present in the moment, without judgment or attachment. It involves paying attention to one's thoughts, emotions, and sensations in a non-reactive way. Mindfulness allows individuals to observe their inner experiences without getting caught up in them, leading to increased self-awareness.

Meditation is a technique that can be used to cultivate mindfulness and self-awareness. It involves sitting in a quiet space and focusing on the breath or a specific object of attention. Through meditation, individuals can develop the ability to observe their thoughts and emotions without getting carried away by them. This leads to a greater understanding of oneself and increased self-awareness.

Embracing Vulnerability: The Key to Authenticity and Self-Awareness

Vulnerability is often seen as a weakness, but it is actually a key component of authenticity and self-awareness. When individuals embrace vulnerability, they allow themselves to be seen and known for who they truly are. This openness and authenticity fosters deeper connections with others and allows individuals to live in alignment with their true selves.

Embracing vulnerability involves taking risks and being willing to be seen, even when it feels uncomfortable. It requires individuals to let go of the need for perfection and embrace their imperfections. By embracing vulnerability, individuals can discover their true selves and experience a greater sense of fulfillment and connection.

The Role of Self-Care in Discovering Your True Self

Self-care is an essential aspect of self-awareness. It involves taking care of one's physical, mental, and emotional well-being. Self-care is important because it allows individuals to prioritize their own needs and recharge their energy.

Practicing self-care is crucial for self-awareness because it allows individuals to tune into their own needs and desires. By taking the time to care for oneself, individuals can gain insight into what brings them joy and fulfillment. This self-awareness enables individuals to make choices that align with their true selves and prioritize activities that nourish their well-being.

The Importance of Self-Compassion: Learning to Love Yourself

Self-compassion is the practice of treating oneself with kindness, understanding, and acceptance. It involves recognizing one's own suffering and responding with compassion and care. Self-compassion is important for self-awareness because it allows individuals to embrace their imperfections and love themselves unconditionally.

Practicing self-compassion involves being kind to oneself, especially in moments of difficulty or failure. It requires individuals to acknowledge their own humanity and treat themselves with the same kindness and understanding they would offer to a loved one. By practicing self-compassion, individuals can cultivate a sense of self-worth and acceptance, leading to increased self-awareness.

Finding Your Purpose: Aligning Your Life with Your True Self

Finding your purpose is an important aspect of self-awareness. When individuals are aware of their values, beliefs, and motivations, they can align their lives with their true selves. This alignment leads to a sense of purpose and fulfillment.

Finding your purpose involves exploring your passions and interests and identifying what brings you joy and fulfillment. It requires individuals to reflect on their values and beliefs and consider how they can contribute to the world in a meaningful way. By finding your purpose, you can live a life that is in alignment with your true self and experience a greater sense of fulfillment.

The Journey to Self-Awareness is a Lifelong Process.

In conclusion, self-awareness is a crucial aspect of personal growth and development. It allows individuals to understand themselves on a deeper level and make informed decisions that align with their true selves. Discovering your true self is important because it allows you to live an authentic life, build healthy relationships, and find fulfillment.

The benefits of self-awareness are numerous, including improved emotional intelligence, better decision-making skills, increased self-confidence, and greater empathy and understanding of others. However, there are obstacles that can hinder the process of self-awareness, such as self-doubt and fear. Overcoming these obstacles requires challenging negative beliefs and embracing vulnerability.

Self-reflection, mindfulness, meditation, self-care, and self-compassion are powerful tools for cultivating self-awareness. They allow individuals to look inward, embrace vulnerability, prioritize their own well-being, and practice kindness towards themselves. Finding your purpose is also important in self-awareness, as it allows individuals to align their lives with their true selves and experience a greater sense of fulfillment.

The journey to self-awareness is a lifelong process. It requires ongoing reflection, practice, and self-compassion. By committing to the journey of self-awareness, individuals can unlock their full potential and live a life that is in alignment with their true selves.

Chapter 8: The Benefits of Positive Thinking: Why It's Worth the Effort

Positive thinking is a mental attitude that focuses on the bright side of life and expects positive outcomes. It involves cultivating a mindset that is optimistic, hopeful, and resilient, even in the face of challenges and setbacks. Positive thinking has a profound impact on mental and emotional health, as well as on daily life.

Research has shown that positive thinking can improve overall well-being and contribute to a happier and more fulfilling life. When we think positively, we are more likely to experience lower levels of stress and anxiety, better physical health, stronger relationships, and increased success in achieving our goals.

Boosting Your Confidence and Self-Esteem with Positive Thoughts

Positive thinking plays a crucial role in boosting self-confidence and self-esteem. When we think positively about ourselves, we develop a belief in our abilities and worthiness. This belief empowers us to take risks, pursue our goals, and overcome obstacles.

One way to cultivate positive self-talk is by using affirmations. Affirmations are positive statements that we repeat to ourselves to reinforce positive beliefs about ourselves. For example, if you struggle with self-doubt, you can repeat affirmations such as "I am capable and deserving of success" or "I believe in myself and my abilities."

Gratitude also plays a significant role in boosting positivity. When we focus on what we are grateful for, we shift our attention away from negative thoughts and towards the positive aspects of our lives. This shift in perspective can help us feel more confident, content, and appreciative of ourselves and our accomplishments.

Overcoming Obstacles and Challenges with a Positive Mindset

A positive mindset is essential for overcoming obstacles and challenges in life. When faced with difficulties, negative thoughts can easily consume us and hinder our ability to find solutions or move forward. However, by adopting a positive mindset, we can reframe negative thoughts and beliefs, allowing us to see challenges as opportunities for growth and learning.

One strategy for reframing negative thoughts is to practice cognitive restructuring. This involves identifying and challenging negative thoughts and replacing them with more positive and realistic ones. For example, if you find yourself thinking, "I'll never be able to do this," you can reframe it as, "I may face challenges, but I am capable of finding solutions and learning from them."

Resilience is another key component of a positive mindset. Resilience is the ability to bounce back from setbacks and adapt to change. By cultivating resilience, we can navigate life's challenges with a positive attitude and a belief in our ability to overcome them.

Improving Your Mental and Emotional Health with Positive Thinking

Positive thinking has a profound impact on mental and emotional health. When we think positively, we experience lower levels of stress and anxiety, improved mood, and increased overall well-being.

One technique for reducing stress and anxiety with positive self-talk is to practice mindfulness. Mindfulness involves paying attention to the present moment without judgment. By practicing mindfulness, we can become aware of our negative thoughts and replace them with more positive and constructive ones.

Positive thinking also plays a crucial role in managing depression and other mental health conditions. When we focus on positive thoughts and beliefs, we can counteract negative thinking patterns that contribute to depression. Additionally, positive thinking can help us develop coping strategies and build resilience in the face of mental health challenges.

Enhancing Your Relationships with Positive Communication and Attitudes

Positive thinking not only improves our relationship with ourselves but also enhances our relationships with others. When we think positively, we are more likely to communicate effectively, resolve conflicts peacefully, and cultivate healthy relationships.

One way to cultivate positive attitudes in relationships is by practicing empathy. Empathy involves putting ourselves in others' shoes and understanding their perspective. By practicing empathy, we can develop a deeper understanding and appreciation for others, leading to more positive and fulfilling relationships.

Another tip for cultivating positive attitudes in relationships is to focus on gratitude. Expressing gratitude towards others can strengthen our relationships and foster a sense of appreciation and connection. By acknowledging and appreciating the positive qualities and actions of others, we can create a more positive and supportive environment.

Achieving Your Goals and Dreams with a Positive Outlook

Positive thinking plays a crucial role in achieving our goals and dreams. When we think positively, we develop a belief in our ability to succeed, which motivates us to take action and persevere in the face of challenges.

One strategy for setting and achieving goals with a positive mindset is to visualize success. Visualization involves mentally picturing ourselves achieving our goals and experiencing the desired outcomes. By visualizing success, we can strengthen our belief in our ability to achieve our goals and increase our motivation to take the necessary steps towards them.

Affirmations also play a powerful role in manifesting success. By repeating positive statements about our goals and abilities, we can reinforce positive beliefs and attract opportunities that align with our desires. For example, if your goal is to start your own business, you can repeat affirmations such as "I am capable of building a successful business" or "I attract abundance and opportunities for growth."

Reducing Stress and Anxiety with Positive Self-Talk and Mindfulness

Positive thinking has a direct impact on stress reduction. When we think positively, we are less likely to dwell on negative thoughts or worry excessively about the future. This shift in mindset allows us to focus on the present moment and approach stressful situations with a calmer and more constructive attitude.

One technique for practicing positive self-talk is to challenge negative thoughts with evidence-based reasoning. For example, if you find yourself thinking, "I can't handle this," you can challenge that thought by reminding yourself of past experiences where you successfully handled similar situations.

Mindfulness meditation is another powerful tool for reducing stress and anxiety. By practicing mindfulness meditation, we can train our minds to focus on the present moment and let go of worries and negative thoughts. This practice allows us to cultivate a sense of calm and inner peace, even in the midst of stressful situations.

Cultivating Resilience and Adaptability with Positive Thinking

Resilience and adaptability are essential qualities for navigating life's challenges. When we think positively, we develop a belief in our ability to overcome obstacles and adapt to change. This positive mindset allows us to bounce back from setbacks and embrace new opportunities.

One strategy for cultivating resilience and adaptability with positive thinking is to practice self-compassion. Self-compassion involves treating ourselves with kindness and understanding, especially during difficult times. By practicing self-compassion, we can develop a more positive and supportive inner dialogue, which strengthens our resilience and ability to adapt.

Positive thinking also plays a crucial role in building emotional intelligence. Emotional intelligence involves the ability to recognize and manage our own emotions, as well as the emotions of others. By cultivating a positive mindset, we can develop greater self-awareness, empathy, and emotional regulation skills, which contribute to our overall resilience and adaptability.

Building a More Fulfilling and Meaningful Life with Positive Thoughts

Positive thinking has the power to transform our lives and lead to greater fulfillment and meaning. When we think positively, we cultivate gratitude, appreciation, and a sense of purpose, which contribute to a more fulfilling and meaningful life.

One way to cultivate gratitude in daily life is by keeping a gratitude journal. Each day, write down three things you are grateful for. This practice helps shift your focus towards the positive aspects of your life and fosters a sense of appreciation for the present moment.

Another tip for building a more fulfilling life with positive thoughts is to focus on your strengths and passions. By identifying and nurturing your strengths and pursuing activities that bring you joy and fulfillment, you can create a life that aligns with your values and aspirations.

Harnessing the Law of Attraction with Positive Visualization and Affirmations

The law of attraction states that like attracts like, meaning that positive thoughts and beliefs attract positive outcomes and experiences. By harnessing the power of positive visualization and affirmations, we can manifest abundance and success in our lives.

Visualization involves mentally picturing ourselves achieving our goals and experiencing the desired outcomes. By visualizing success, we create a clear image of what we want to attract into our lives, which helps align our thoughts, beliefs, and actions with our desires.

Affirmations also play a crucial role in harnessing the law of attraction. By repeating positive statements about our goals and desires, we reinforce positive beliefs and attract opportunities that align with our intentions. For example, if your goal is to find a loving relationship, you can repeat affirmations such as "I am worthy of love and attract a loving partner" or "I am open to receiving love and creating a fulfilling relationship."

Embracing the Benefits of Positive Thinking for a Happier Life

In conclusion, positive thinking has a profound impact on our mental, emotional, and overall well-being. By cultivating a positive mindset, we can boost our confidence and self-esteem, overcome obstacles and challenges, improve our relationships, achieve our goals and dreams, reduce stress and anxiety, build resilience and adaptability, create a more fulfilling life, and harness the law of attraction.

It is important to remember that positive thinking is not about denying or ignoring negative emotions or experiences. Instead, it is about acknowledging them while choosing to focus on the positive aspects of life. By embracing the benefits of positive thinking and incorporating it into our daily lives, we can create a happier and more fulfilling life for ourselves and those around us.

Chapter 9: Mastering Emotional Intelligence: The Key to Success in Life and Business

Emotional intelligence is a term that has gained significant attention in recent years, and for good reason. It refers to the ability to recognize, understand, and manage our own emotions, as well as the emotions of others. This skill is crucial in both our personal and professional lives, as it affects our relationships, decision-making abilities, and overall well-being. In this article, we will explore the concept of emotional intelligence in depth, discussing its importance, components, and strategies for development.

What is Emotional Intelligence and Why is it Important?

Emotional intelligence can be defined as the ability to recognize and understand our own emotions, as well as the emotions of others. It involves being aware of how our emotions impact our thoughts and behaviors, and being able to regulate those emotions effectively. Additionally, emotional intelligence encompasses empathy, or the ability to understand and share the feelings of others.

Emotional intelligence is important because it affects every aspect of our lives. In our personal lives, it helps us build strong relationships, resolve conflicts effectively, and communicate with others in a meaningful way. In our professional lives, emotional intelligence is crucial for effective leadership, teamwork, and decision-making. Research has shown that individuals with high emotional intelligence are more likely to succeed in their careers and experience greater job satisfaction.

The Five Components of Emotional Intelligence

Emotional intelligence can be broken down into five components: self-awareness, self-regulation, motivation, empathy, and social skills.

Self-awareness involves recognizing and understanding our own emotions. It requires being able to accurately identify how we feel in different situations and understanding the impact those emotions have on our thoughts and behaviors.

Self-regulation refers to the ability to manage our emotions effectively. It involves controlling impulsive behaviors, managing stress, and adapting to changing circumstances.

Motivation is the drive to achieve goals and pursue success. Individuals with high emotional intelligence are often motivated by a desire to improve themselves and make a positive impact on others.

Empathy is the ability to understand and share the feelings of others. It involves being able to put ourselves in someone else's shoes and respond with compassion and understanding.

Social skills refer to the ability to build and maintain relationships. This includes effective communication, conflict resolution, and teamwork.

How to Develop Self-Awareness and Self-Regulation

Developing self-awareness is a crucial first step in improving emotional intelligence. Here are some tips for developing self-awareness:

1. Practice mindfulness: Take time each day to focus on the present moment and observe your thoughts and emotions without judgment.

2. Keep a journal: Write down your thoughts and feelings regularly to gain insight into your emotions and patterns of behavior.

3. Seek feedback: Ask trusted friends or family members for honest feedback about how you come across in different situations.

4. Reflect on past experiences: Take time to reflect on past experiences and consider how your emotions influenced your actions and decisions.

Improving self-regulation requires practice and self-discipline. Here are some strategies for improving self-regulation:

1. Identify triggers: Pay attention to situations or events that tend to trigger strong emotional reactions in you. Once you are aware of these triggers, you can develop strategies for managing them effectively.

2. Take a pause: When you feel yourself becoming overwhelmed with emotion, take a moment to pause and collect yourself before responding.

3. Practice relaxation techniques: Engage in activities such as deep breathing, meditation, or exercise to help calm your mind and body when you are feeling stressed or anxious.

4. Set goals: Set realistic goals for yourself and develop a plan for achieving them. This can help you stay focused and motivated, even when faced with challenges.

Improving Your Empathy and Social Skills

Empathy is a skill that can be developed with practice. Here are some techniques for improving empathy:

1. Listen actively: When someone is speaking to you, give them your full attention and listen without interrupting. Try to understand their perspective and validate their feelings.

2. Practice perspective-taking: Put yourself in someone else's shoes and try to imagine how they might be feeling in a particular situation.

3. Show compassion: Express empathy and understanding when someone is going through a difficult time. Offer support and reassurance.

Enhancing social skills involves effective communication, conflict resolution, and teamwork. Here are some ways to enhance your social skills:

1. Practice active listening: Pay attention to both verbal and non-verbal cues when communicating with others. Show that you are engaged and interested in what they have to say.

2. Develop assertiveness: Learn to express your thoughts and feelings in a clear and respectful manner. Practice assertive communication techniques, such as using "I" statements and expressing your needs and boundaries.

3. Collaborate with others: Seek opportunities to work collaboratively with others, whether it be on a project at work or a group activity outside of work. Practice compromising, sharing ideas, and working towards a common goal.

The Importance of Emotional Intelligence in Leadership

Emotional intelligence is particularly important in leadership roles. Leaders with high emotional intelligence are able to inspire and motivate their team members, build strong relationships, and make sound decisions. They are also able to effectively manage conflicts and navigate challenging situations.

Leaders who possess emotional intelligence are often seen as approachable and trustworthy, which fosters open communication and collaboration within the team. They are able to understand the needs and concerns of their team members, which allows them to provide the necessary support and guidance.

Examples of successful leaders with high emotional intelligence include Oprah Winfrey, who is known for her ability to connect with others on an emotional level, and Nelson Mandela, who demonstrated empathy and forgiveness throughout his leadership journey.

How Emotional Intelligence Can Improve Your Relationships

Emotional intelligence plays a crucial role in building and maintaining healthy relationships. It allows us to understand and respond to the emotions of others, which fosters empathy and connection. Here are some ways in which emotional intelligence can enhance personal relationships:

1. Improved communication: Individuals with high emotional intelligence are able to communicate effectively and express their thoughts and feelings in a clear and respectful manner. This leads to better understanding and fewer misunderstandings.

2. Conflict resolution: Emotional intelligence helps individuals navigate conflicts in a constructive way. It allows them to understand the perspectives of others, find common ground, and work towards a resolution that satisfies everyone involved.

3. Empathy and understanding: Emotional intelligence enables individuals to understand and share the feelings of their loved ones. This fosters a sense of connection and support, which is essential for healthy relationships.

Tips for improving communication and resolving conflicts include active listening, using "I" statements, and seeking to understand before being understood.

Overcoming Emotional Triggers and Reacting Positively

Emotional triggers are events or situations that elicit strong emotional reactions in us. They can be anything from a certain word or phrase to a specific behavior or situation. Understanding our emotional triggers is important because it allows us to react in a more positive and constructive manner.

To overcome emotional triggers, it is important to first identify them. Pay attention to situations or events that consistently elicit strong emotional reactions in you. Once you have identified your triggers, you can develop strategies for reacting positively:

1. Take a step back: When you feel yourself becoming triggered, take a step back and give yourself some space. This will allow you to collect your thoughts and respond in a more rational manner.

2. Practice self-care: Engage in activities that help you relax and reduce stress, such as exercise, meditation, or spending time in nature. Taking care of your physical and mental well-being can help you better manage emotional triggers.

3. Reframe your thoughts: Challenge negative or irrational thoughts that may be contributing to your emotional reactions. Replace them with more positive and realistic thoughts.

How to Manage Stress and Anxiety with Emotional Intelligence

Emotional intelligence can be a powerful tool for managing stress and anxiety. Here are some ways in which emotional intelligence can help:

1. Recognize and understand your emotions: Emotional intelligence allows you to recognize when you are feeling stressed or anxious, and understand the impact those emotions have on your thoughts and behaviors.

2. Practice self-regulation: Emotional intelligence helps you regulate your emotions effectively, which can help reduce stress and anxiety. Techniques such as deep breathing, meditation, and exercise can be helpful in managing these emotions.

3. Seek support: Emotional intelligence involves recognizing when you need support and reaching out to others for help. Talk to a trusted friend or family member about what you are experiencing, or consider seeking professional help if needed.

The Benefits of Emotional Intelligence in the Workplace

Emotional intelligence is highly valued in the workplace because it has been shown to improve workplace relationships, productivity, and overall job satisfaction. Here are some ways in which emotional intelligence can benefit the workplace:

1. Improved communication: Individuals with high emotional intelligence are able to communicate effectively with their colleagues, leading to better understanding and collaboration.

2. Conflict resolution: Emotional intelligence helps individuals navigate conflicts in a constructive manner, leading to more positive outcomes and stronger relationships.

3. Leadership effectiveness: Leaders with high emotional intelligence are able to inspire and motivate their team members, leading to increased productivity and job satisfaction.

Examples of companies that prioritize emotional intelligence include Google, which offers emotional intelligence training to its employees, and Zappos, which values empathy and emotional connection with customers.

How to Teach Emotional Intelligence to Children and Teens

Teaching emotional intelligence to children and teens is important for their overall well-being and success in life. Here are some tips for teaching emotional intelligence:

1. Model emotional intelligence: Children learn by observing the behavior of adults around them. Model emotional intelligence by expressing your own emotions in a healthy way and demonstrating empathy towards others.

2. Encourage emotional expression: Create a safe and supportive environment where children feel comfortable expressing their emotions. Encourage them to talk about how they feel and validate their emotions.

3. Teach problem-solving skills: Help children develop problem-solving skills by encouraging them to think through different solutions to a problem and consider the potential consequences of each option.

Resources for parents and educators include books such as "The Whole-Brain Child" by Daniel J. Siegel and Tina Payne Bryson, and online courses or workshops on emotional intelligence.

The Future of Emotional Intelligence: Trends and Predictions

The field of emotional intelligence is constantly evolving, with new research and trends emerging. Some of the current trends in emotional intelligence research include:

1. Artificial intelligence: Researchers are exploring the use of artificial intelligence to assess and develop emotional intelligence skills. This includes the use of virtual reality simulations and chatbots.

2. Emotional intelligence in technology: There is a growing focus on incorporating emotional intelligence into technology, such as virtual assistants or chatbots that can recognize and respond to human emotions.

3. Emotional intelligence in education: There is an increasing recognition of the importance of teaching emotional intelligence in schools. Many educators are incorporating social-emotional learning programs into their curriculum.

Predictions for the future of emotional intelligence include increased integration into workplace training programs, advancements in technology that can assess and develop emotional intelligence skills, and a greater emphasis on teaching emotional intelligence in schools.

Emotional intelligence is a crucial skill that impacts every aspect of our lives. It allows us to understand and manage our own emotions, as well as the emotions of others. By developing our emotional intelligence, we can improve our relationships, make better decisions, and enhance our overall well-being. Whether in our personal or professional lives, emotional intelligence is a skill that can be learned and developed with practice. So, let us commit to improving our emotional intelligence and reaping the benefits it brings.

Chapter 10: Unlocking the Secret to Unstoppable Motivation: Tips from Top Performers

Motivation is a key factor in achieving success in any area of life. Whether it's pursuing a career goal, maintaining a healthy lifestyle, or working towards personal growth, motivation plays a crucial role in keeping us focused and driven. In this article, we will explore various aspects of motivation and provide practical tips and strategies to help you stay motivated and achieve your goals.

The Power of Purpose: How to Find Your Why and Stay Motivated

Having a clear purpose is essential for staying motivated. When we have a strong sense of why we are doing something, it becomes easier to stay committed and overcome obstacles along the way. To discover your purpose, take some time to reflect on your values, passions, and what brings you joy. Consider what impact you want to make in the world and how you can align your goals with your values.

Once you have identified your purpose, it's important to remind yourself of it regularly. Write it down and place it somewhere visible, such as on your desk or bathroom mirror. Whenever you feel demotivated or face challenges, remind yourself of your purpose and how it aligns with your goals. This will help you stay focused and motivated even during difficult times.

From Procrastination to Productivity: Tips for Overcoming Laziness

Procrastination is a common obstacle to motivation and productivity. It can be caused by various factors such as fear of failure, lack of clarity, or feeling overwhelmed. To overcome laziness and increase productivity, it's important to identify the root cause of your procrastination.

One strategy is to break tasks down into smaller, more manageable steps. This helps to reduce overwhelm and makes the task feel more achievable. Set specific deadlines for each step and hold yourself accountable to them.

Another strategy is to create a productive environment. Remove distractions such as social media notifications or clutter from your workspace. Set clear boundaries with others and communicate your need for uninterrupted time to focus on your tasks.

The Role of Habits in Motivation: How to Build a Routine That Works for You

Habits play a significant role in motivation. When we have established positive habits, they become automatic and require less willpower to maintain. Building a routine that supports your goals is essential for staying motivated.

Start by identifying the habits that will help you achieve your goals. For example, if your goal is to exercise regularly, establish a habit of going to the gym or taking a walk every morning. Start small and gradually increase the intensity or duration of the habit.

To make it easier to stick to your routine, create cues and triggers that remind you to perform the habit. For example, if you want to develop a habit of reading every night before bed, place a book on your nightstand as a visual reminder.

Mind over Matter: Strategies for Overcoming Mental Barriers to Success

Our mindset plays a significant role in our motivation and ability to achieve success. Negative self-talk and limiting beliefs can hinder our progress and hold us back from reaching our full potential.

To overcome mental barriers, it's important to become aware of your thoughts and challenge any negative or limiting beliefs. Replace them with positive affirmations and focus on your strengths and past successes.

Practice visualization techniques to imagine yourself achieving your goals and experiencing success. This can help boost your confidence and motivation.

Fueling Your Fire: How to Stay Energized and Focused Throughout the Day

Maintaining energy and focus throughout the day is crucial for staying motivated. There are several strategies you can implement to ensure you have the energy and mental clarity needed to stay motivated.

Firstly, prioritize self-care. Get enough sleep, eat nutritious meals, and engage in regular exercise. Taking care of your physical health will provide you with the energy needed to stay motivated.

Secondly, take regular breaks throughout the day. Allow yourself time to rest and recharge. This can be as simple as taking a short walk outside or practicing deep breathing exercises.

Lastly, manage your stress levels. High levels of stress can drain your energy and motivation. Practice stress management techniques such as meditation, journaling, or engaging in hobbies that bring you joy.

The Importance of Self-Care: How to Prioritize Your Well-Being for Optimal Performance

Self-care is often overlooked when it comes to motivation and success. However, taking care of your well-being is essential for optimal performance and staying motivated.

Make self-care a priority by scheduling regular time for activities that bring you joy and relaxation. This could be anything from taking a bubble bath, reading a book, or spending time with loved ones.

Practice self-compassion and be kind to yourself. Acknowledge your achievements and celebrate your progress, no matter how small.

The Benefits of Accountability: How to Stay on Track with a Support System

Accountability is a powerful tool for staying motivated and achieving goals. Having someone to hold you accountable can provide support, encouragement, and help you stay on track.

Find an accountability partner or join a support group where you can share your goals and progress. Set regular check-ins with your accountability partner to discuss your progress and any challenges you may be facing.

The Art of Goal-Setting: How to Set Realistic Targets and Achieve Them

Setting realistic goals is crucial for staying motivated. When goals are too vague or unrealistic, it can be demotivating and lead to feelings of failure.

Set specific, measurable, achievable, relevant, and time-bound (SMART) goals. Break them down into smaller milestones that are easier to achieve and track your progress along the way.

Celebrate each milestone reached to maintain motivation and momentum towards your larger goal.

Embracing Failure: How to Learn from Setbacks and Keep Moving Forward

Failure is a natural part of the journey towards success. Instead of viewing failure as a setback, reframe it as a learning opportunity.

Reflect on what went wrong and identify the lessons learned. Use this knowledge to adjust your approach and keep moving forward.

Maintain a growth mindset and view failure as a stepping stone towards success. Remember that every successful person has faced setbacks along the way.

The Power of Positive Thinking: How to Harness Optimism for Motivation

Positive thinking is a powerful tool for motivation. When we have a positive mindset, we are more likely to believe in our abilities and stay motivated.

Practice gratitude by focusing on the things you are grateful for each day. This can help shift your mindset towards positivity and increase motivation.

Surround yourself with positive influences such as uplifting books, podcasts, or inspirational quotes. These can serve as reminders to stay positive and motivated.

Finding Inspiration in Unlikely Places: How to Stay Motivated When the Going Gets Tough

During difficult times, it can be challenging to stay motivated. However, inspiration can be found in unlikely places if we are open to it.

Seek out stories of resilience and success from others who have overcome similar challenges. This can provide motivation and remind you that you are not alone in your journey.

Look for inspiration in nature, art, or music. These sources can evoke emotions and spark creativity, which can help reignite your motivation.

Motivation is essential for achieving success in any area of life. By understanding the power of purpose, overcoming laziness, building positive habits, overcoming mental barriers, prioritizing self-care, embracing accountability, setting realistic goals, learning from failure, harnessing positive thinking, finding inspiration in unlikely places, and implementing the strategies discussed in this article, you can stay motivated and achieve your goals. Remember that motivation is not a one-time fix, but a continuous process that requires effort and commitment. Stay focused, stay motivated, and keep moving forward towards your dreams.

Chapter 11: Unleashing the Power Within: How to Tap into Your Inner Strength

Inner strength is a powerful and essential quality that can greatly impact our lives. It is the ability to stay resilient, persevere through challenges, and maintain a positive mindset. Developing inner strength allows us to overcome self-doubt and fear, set achievable goals, take action towards our dreams, and nurture our physical health and well-being. In this article, we will explore the concept of inner strength and provide practical tips on how to cultivate it in our lives.

Understanding the concept of inner strength

Inner strength can be defined as the mental and emotional fortitude that enables individuals to face adversity with courage and resilience. It is the ability to stay grounded and maintain a positive mindset even in the face of challenges. Inner strength is not something we are born with, but rather something that can be developed and nurtured over time.

Developing inner strength is important because it allows us to navigate through life's ups and downs with grace and resilience. It helps us overcome obstacles, bounce back from failures, and stay focused on our goals. Inner strength also plays a crucial role in maintaining our mental health and well-being. When we have a strong inner foundation, we are better equipped to handle stress, manage our emotions, and cultivate a positive outlook on life.

Identifying your personal sources of inner strength

Everyone has their own unique sources of inner strength. These sources can vary from person to person, but they often include qualities such as resilience, determination, faith, love, and self-belief. Some people may find strength in their relationships with loved ones, while others may draw strength from their spirituality or personal values.

To identify your personal sources of inner strength, take some time for self-reflection. Think about the times when you felt most empowered and resilient. What qualities or beliefs helped you get through those challenging moments? Consider your values, passions, and the people who inspire you. These can all be sources of inner strength that you can tap into when faced with difficulties.

Overcoming self-doubt and fear

Self-doubt and fear are common obstacles that can hinder our inner strength. They can hold us back from pursuing our dreams and reaching our full potential. Overcoming self-doubt and fear requires a combination of self-awareness, self-compassion, and taking small steps outside of our comfort zone.

One way to overcome self-doubt is to challenge negative thoughts and beliefs. Replace self-critical thoughts with positive affirmations and remind yourself of your past successes and strengths. Surround yourself with supportive and encouraging people who believe in you and your abilities.

To overcome fear, it is important to take small steps outside of your comfort zone. Start by setting small goals or taking on new challenges that push you slightly out of your comfort zone. Celebrate each small victory along the way, as this will help build your confidence and strengthen your inner resilience.

Cultivating a positive mindset

A positive mindset is a key component of inner strength. It allows us to approach challenges with optimism, see setbacks as opportunities for growth, and maintain a sense of gratitude and appreciation for life. Cultivating a positive mindset requires conscious effort and practice.

One strategy for cultivating a positive mindset is to practice gratitude. Take time each day to reflect on the things you are grateful for, no matter how small they may seem. This can help shift your focus from what is going wrong to what is going right in your life.

Another strategy is to reframe negative thoughts into positive ones. When faced with a setback or challenge, try to find the silver lining or the lesson that can be learned from the experience. This can help you maintain a positive outlook and keep moving forward.

Building resilience and perseverance

Resilience and perseverance are essential qualities for developing inner strength. Resilience is the ability to bounce back from setbacks and adapt to change, while perseverance is the ability to stay committed to your goals despite obstacles and setbacks.

To build resilience, it is important to develop a growth mindset. Embrace challenges as opportunities for growth and learning, rather than viewing them as failures. Practice self-care and stress management techniques to help you cope with adversity and bounce back stronger.

To cultivate perseverance, set clear goals and break them down into smaller, manageable steps. Celebrate each small milestone along the way, as this will help keep you motivated and focused on your long-term goals. Surround yourself with supportive people who can provide encouragement and accountability.

Setting achievable goals

Setting achievable goals is an important aspect of developing inner strength. When we have clear goals in mind, we are more likely to stay focused, motivated, and resilient in the face of challenges.

When setting goals, it is important to make them specific, measurable, attainable, relevant, and time-bound (SMART). This means setting goals that are clear and specific, measurable so that progress can be tracked, attainable so that they are within reach, relevant to your values and aspirations, and time-bound with a deadline.

Break down your larger goals into smaller, actionable steps that can be taken on a daily or weekly basis. This will make your goals more manageable and increase your chances of success. Regularly review and adjust your goals as needed to ensure they remain relevant and aligned with your aspirations.

Taking action towards your goals

Taking action is a crucial step in developing inner strength. It is not enough to simply set goals; you must also take consistent action towards achieving them.

To take action towards your goals, start by breaking them down into smaller tasks or action steps. Prioritize these tasks based on their importance and urgency. Create a schedule or action plan that outlines when and how you will complete each task.

Hold yourself accountable by setting deadlines and tracking your progress. Celebrate each small accomplishment along the way, as this will help keep you motivated and reinforce your inner strength.

Nurturing your physical health and well-being

Physical health and well-being are foundational to developing inner strength. When we take care of our bodies, we have more energy, mental clarity, and resilience to face life's challenges.

To nurture your physical health and well-being, prioritize self-care activities such as exercise, healthy eating, and getting enough sleep. Engage in activities that bring you joy and help you relax, such as hobbies, spending time in nature, or practicing mindfulness.

Take breaks throughout the day to stretch, move your body, and clear your mind. Practice stress management techniques such as deep breathing, meditation, or journaling to help reduce stress and promote overall well-being.

Building a support system

Building a support system is essential for developing inner strength. Surrounding yourself with positive and supportive people can provide encouragement, guidance, and accountability on your journey towards personal growth.

To build a support system, seek out like-minded individuals who share similar goals or interests. Join clubs, organizations, or online communities where you can connect with others who are on a similar path. Attend workshops or seminars where you can learn from experts in your field of interest.

Be open to receiving support and guidance from others. Share your goals and aspirations with trusted friends or family members who can provide encouragement and hold you accountable. Offer support to others in return, as this will strengthen your relationships and create a sense of community.

Embracing failure as a learning opportunity

Embracing failure is an important aspect of developing inner strength. Failure is not a reflection of our worth or abilities; rather, it is an opportunity for growth and learning.

To embrace failure as a learning opportunity, shift your mindset from viewing failure as a negative outcome to seeing it as a stepping stone towards success. Reflect on what went wrong and what lessons can be learned from the experience. Use failure as motivation to improve and try again.

Practice self-compassion and remind yourself that everyone makes mistakes and experiences setbacks. Treat yourself with kindness and understanding, just as you would a close friend or loved one. Embrace failure as a natural part of the learning process and use it to fuel your inner strength.

Celebrating your achievements and progress

Celebrating your achievements and progress is an important aspect of developing inner strength. Recognizing and acknowledging your accomplishments can boost your confidence, motivation, and overall sense of well-being.

To celebrate your achievements, set aside time to reflect on your progress and give yourself credit for the hard work you have put in. Take note of the skills you have developed, the obstacles you have overcome, and the growth you have experienced along the way.

Reward yourself for reaching milestones or accomplishing goals. Treat yourself to something special, whether it's a small indulgence or a meaningful experience. Share your achievements with loved ones who can provide support and celebrate with you.

Developing inner strength is a lifelong journey that requires self-awareness, practice, and perseverance. By understanding the concept of inner strength, identifying our personal sources of strength, overcoming self-doubt and fear, cultivating a positive mindset, building resilience and perseverance, setting achievable goals, taking action towards our goals, nurturing our physical health and well-being, building a support system, embracing failure as a learning opportunity, and celebrating our achievements and progress, we can cultivate inner strength that will empower us to navigate through life's challenges with grace and resilience. Remember that developing inner strength is not about being perfect or never experiencing difficulties; it is about having the tools and mindset to bounce back stronger each time we face adversity.

Chapter 13: The Art of Authenticity: How to Embrace Your Unique Self

Authenticity is a quality that is highly valued in today's society. It refers to being true to oneself, embracing one's unique qualities, and living in alignment with one's values and beliefs. In a world that often encourages conformity and fakeness, authenticity stands out as a powerful force for personal growth and fulfillment. This article will explore the concept of authenticity, its importance, and how it can improve various aspects of our lives.

Understanding Authenticity: What Does It Mean to be Authentic?

Authenticity can be defined as the genuine expression of one's true self. It involves being honest and transparent about who you are, what you believe in, and what you stand for. It means not pretending to be someone you're not or conforming to societal expectations just to fit in.

Authenticity is often confused with conformity or fakeness. Conformity is the act of changing oneself to fit in with a particular group or society, even if it goes against one's true nature. Fakeness, on the other hand, involves pretending to be someone or something that you're not in order to gain acceptance or approval.

The Power of Embracing Your Unique Self: Why Authenticity Matters

Embracing one's unique self and living authentically can have numerous benefits. When we are true to ourselves, we experience a sense of freedom and liberation. We no longer feel the need to hide or pretend, and we can fully express our thoughts, feelings, and desires.

Authenticity also allows us to build deeper and more meaningful connections with others. When we are authentic, we attract people who appreciate us for who we truly are, rather than for who we pretend to be. This leads to more fulfilling relationships and a stronger sense of belonging.

There are many successful people who have embraced their authenticity and achieved great things as a result. For example, Oprah Winfrey is known for her authenticity and vulnerability in sharing her personal struggles and triumphs. This has allowed her to connect with millions of people and build a media empire. Similarly, Steve Jobs was known for his authenticity and passion for his work, which led to the success of Apple Inc.

The Benefits of Being Authentic: How It Can Improve Your Life

Embracing authenticity can have a profound impact on our lives. One of the key benefits is improved self-esteem and self-confidence. When we are true to ourselves, we no longer feel the need to seek validation or approval from others. We become more comfortable in our own skin and develop a stronger sense of self-worth.

Authenticity also leads to better relationships and connections. When we are authentic, we attract people who appreciate us for who we truly are, rather than for who we pretend to be. This leads to more fulfilling relationships and a stronger sense of belonging.

Furthermore, embracing authenticity can increase our creativity and productivity. When we are true to ourselves, we are more likely to pursue activities and projects that align with our passions and interests.

This leads to a greater sense of fulfillment and motivation, which in turn enhances our creativity and productivity.

The Challenges of Being Authentic: Overcoming Fear and Self-Doubt

While embracing authenticity can be incredibly rewarding, it is not without its challenges. One of the common fears associated with authenticity is the fear of judgment or rejection. When we show our true selves, we open ourselves up to criticism and disapproval from others. This fear can hold us back from fully embracing our authenticity.

Another challenge is self-doubt. We may question whether our true selves are worthy or valuable enough. We may worry that if we show our flaws or vulnerabilities, others will see us as weak or inadequate. These doubts can prevent us from fully embracing our authenticity.

To overcome these challenges, it is important to cultivate self-compassion and self-acceptance. We need to remind ourselves that we are worthy and valuable just as we are, flaws and all. It can also be helpful to surround ourselves with supportive and accepting people who encourage us to be authentic.

The Role of Vulnerability in Authenticity: Why It's Okay to Show Your Flaws

Vulnerability is an essential component of authenticity. It involves being open and honest about our weaknesses, fears, and insecurities. While vulnerability can be uncomfortable, it is necessary for building genuine connections with others.

When we show our flaws and vulnerabilities, we allow others to see us as human beings with struggles and imperfections. This creates a sense of empathy and understanding, which in turn strengthens our relationships. It also allows us to grow and learn from our experiences, as we are able to acknowledge and address our weaknesses.

The Importance of Self-Awareness: How to Identify Your Authentic Self

Self-awareness is a crucial step in embracing authenticity. It involves understanding who we truly are, what we value, and what brings us joy and fulfillment. Without self-awareness, it is difficult to live authentically.

There are several steps we can take to become more self-aware. One approach is self-reflection, which involves taking the time to introspect and examine our thoughts, feelings, and behaviors. Journaling, meditation, and therapy can also be helpful tools for self-discovery.

Additionally, there are many resources available for self-discovery, such as personality assessments and career tests. These tools can provide valuable insights into our strengths, weaknesses, and interests, helping us to better understand ourselves.

The Art of Self-Expression: Finding Your Voice and Sharing Your Story

Self-expression is a key aspect of authenticity. It involves finding our unique voice and sharing our story with the world. When we express ourselves authentically, we allow others to see and appreciate our true selves.

Finding our voice and sharing our story can be a challenging process. It requires us to dig deep and uncover our passions, values, and beliefs. It also requires us to overcome any fears or doubts that may hold us back from expressing ourselves.

One way to find our voice is through creative outlets such as writing, art, or music. These activities allow us to express ourselves in a unique and authentic way. It can also be helpful to surround ourselves with supportive and encouraging people who appreciate and value our authentic expression.

The Impact of Social Media on Authenticity: Navigating the Pressure to Conform

Social media has become a powerful platform for self-expression, but it can also pose challenges to authenticity. The pressure to conform and present a perfect image can be overwhelming, leading many people to hide their true selves or pretend to be someone they're not.

To stay true to oneself on social media, it is important to remember that what we see online is often a curated version of reality. People tend to highlight the positive aspects of their lives and hide their struggles and flaws. It is important not to compare ourselves to these idealized images and instead focus on being authentic and true to ourselves.

Setting boundaries with social media can also be helpful. This may involve limiting the amount of time spent on social media or unfollowing accounts that make us feel inadequate or inauthentic. It can also be beneficial to engage in offline activities that bring us joy and fulfillment, allowing us to connect with our authentic selves.

The Role of Authenticity in Relationships: How to Build Genuine Connections

Authenticity plays a crucial role in building genuine connections with others. When we are authentic, we attract people who appreciate us for who we truly are, rather than for who we pretend to be. This leads to more fulfilling relationships based on trust, understanding, and acceptance.

To be authentic in relationships, it is important to communicate openly and honestly. This involves expressing our thoughts, feelings, and desires in a genuine and transparent way. It also involves actively listening to others and being present in the moment.

It is also important to set boundaries and prioritize self-care in relationships. This means being true to ourselves and not compromising our values or beliefs for the sake of pleasing others. It also means taking care of our own needs and well-being, rather than constantly sacrificing ourselves for the sake of the relationship.

The Connection Between Authenticity and Success: How Being True to Yourself Can Help You Achieve Your Goals

There is a strong connection between authenticity and success. When we are true to ourselves, we are more likely to pursue activities and projects that align with our passions and interests. This leads to a greater sense of fulfillment and motivation, which in turn enhances our creativity and productivity.

Authenticity also allows us to build stronger relationships and connections, which can open doors to new opportunities and collaborations. When we are authentic, we attract people who appreciate us for who we truly are, rather than for who we pretend to be. This leads to more meaningful connections that can support us in achieving our goals.

There are many successful people who have embraced their authenticity and achieved great things as a result. For example, Brené Brown is known for her authenticity and vulnerability in her research on shame, vulnerability, and courage. Her TED Talk on vulnerability has been viewed millions of times and has led to numerous speaking engagements and book deals.

The Journey to Authenticity: Tips and Strategies for Embracing Your Unique Self

Embracing authenticity is a journey that requires self-reflection, self-acceptance, and courage. Here are some practical tips and strategies for embracing your unique self:

1. Practice self-reflection: Take the time to introspect and examine your thoughts, feelings, and behaviors. Journaling, meditation, and therapy can be helpful tools for self-discovery.

2. Surround yourself with supportive people: Seek out relationships and connections with people who appreciate and value your authentic self. Avoid toxic or judgmental individuals who may discourage you from being true to yourself.

3. Set boundaries: Prioritize self-care and set boundaries in your relationships and interactions. Be true to yourself and do not compromise your values or beliefs for the sake of pleasing others.

4. Embrace vulnerability: Allow yourself to be open and honest about your weaknesses, fears, and insecurities. This creates a sense of empathy and understanding, which in turn strengthens your relationships.

5. Find your voice: Explore creative outlets such as writing, art, or music to express yourself authentically. Surround yourself with supportive and encouraging people who appreciate and value your authentic expression.

Authenticity is a powerful force for personal growth and fulfillment. It involves being true to oneself, embracing one's unique qualities, and living in alignment with one's values and beliefs. Embracing authenticity can lead to improved self-esteem, better relationships, increased creativity, and a greater sense of fulfillment.

While embracing authenticity can be challenging, it is a journey worth taking. By cultivating self-awareness, embracing vulnerability, and finding our voice, we can live more authentic lives and build genuine connections with others. In a world that often encourages conformity and fakeness, authenticity stands out as a beacon of light and truth. So let us embrace our unique selves and live authentically, for it is in our authenticity that we find our truest selves.

Chapter 13: Rising Above: How to Overcome Obstacles and Achieve Your Goals

Overcoming obstacles is a crucial aspect of achieving success in both our personal and professional lives. Whether it's a challenging project at work, a difficult relationship, or a personal goal we want to achieve, obstacles are inevitable. However, it is how we approach and overcome these obstacles that truly determines our level of success.

Obstacles can come in many forms, such as fear, self-doubt, lack of resources, or external circumstances beyond our control. They can hinder our progress and make us feel stuck or overwhelmed. However, by recognizing and addressing these obstacles head-on, we can develop the resilience and determination needed to overcome them.

Identifying Your Obstacles: Recognizing What's Holding You Back

The first step in overcoming obstacles is to identify what is holding you back. This requires self-reflection and an honest assessment of your strengths and weaknesses. Take the time to reflect on your personal and professional life and identify any recurring patterns or challenges that you face.

Once you have identified your obstacles, it is important to analyze them. Ask yourself why these obstacles exist and what impact they have on your life. Are they internal or external? Are they based on limiting beliefs or lack of resources? By understanding the root causes of your obstacles, you can begin to develop strategies to overcome them.

Setting Realistic Goals: Defining What You Want to Achieve

Setting realistic goals is essential in overcoming obstacles. Without clear goals, it can be difficult to stay focused and motivated when faced with challenges. When setting goals, it is important to make them specific, measurable, achievable, relevant, and time-bound (SMART).

Specific goals provide clarity on what you want to achieve. Measurable goals allow you to track your progress and determine if you are on track. Achievable goals ensure that they are within your reach and not too overwhelming. Relevant goals align with your values and aspirations. Time-bound goals have a deadline, which creates a sense of urgency and helps you stay focused.

Developing a Positive Mindset: Cultivating a Can-Do Attitude

A positive mindset is crucial in overcoming obstacles. It allows you to approach challenges with optimism and resilience. Cultivating a positive mindset involves shifting your perspective and focusing on solutions rather than problems.

One way to develop a positive mindset is through positive self-talk. Replace negative thoughts with positive affirmations and remind yourself of your strengths and past successes. Surround yourself with positive influences, such as supportive friends or mentors, who can help you maintain a positive outlook.

Another way to cultivate a positive mindset is through gratitude. Take the time to appreciate the things you have accomplished and the lessons you have learned along the way. By focusing on the positives, you can overcome obstacles with a can-do attitude.

Building Resilience: Bouncing Back from Setbacks

Resilience is the ability to bounce back from setbacks and adapt to change. It is an essential trait in overcoming obstacles and achieving success. Building resilience involves developing coping mechanisms and strategies to deal with adversity.

One way to build resilience is through self-care. Take care of your physical, mental, and emotional well-being by getting enough sleep, eating nutritious food, exercising regularly, and practicing relaxation techniques such as meditation or deep breathing exercises.

Another way to build resilience is by reframing setbacks as learning opportunities. Instead of viewing failures as permanent or personal, see them as stepping stones towards growth and improvement. Learn from your mistakes and use them as motivation to keep moving forward.

Creating a Plan of Action: Mapping Out Your Path to Success

Having a plan of action is crucial in overcoming obstacles. It provides a roadmap for achieving your goals and helps you stay focused and motivated along the way. When creating a plan of action, break down your goals into smaller, manageable tasks.

Start by identifying the steps you need to take to achieve your goals. Then, prioritize these steps based on their importance and urgency. Set deadlines for each task to create a sense of accountability and ensure that you stay on track.

It is also important to anticipate potential obstacles and develop contingency plans. By thinking ahead and preparing for challenges, you can overcome them more effectively when they arise. Flexibility is key in adapting your plan as needed and making adjustments along the way.

Cultivating Discipline: Staying Focused and Motivated

Discipline is essential in achieving your goals and overcoming obstacles. It requires self-control, consistency, and the ability to stay focused even when faced with distractions or setbacks. Cultivating discipline involves developing habits and routines that support your goals.

One way to cultivate discipline is by setting daily or weekly targets. Break down your goals into smaller, manageable tasks and commit to completing them each day or week. This creates a sense of momentum and progress, which can help you stay motivated.

Another way to cultivate discipline is by eliminating distractions. Identify any habits or activities that are taking up your time and energy without contributing to your goals. Limit your exposure to these distractions and create a conducive environment for focus and productivity.

Seeking Support: Finding the Right People to Help You Succeed

Having a support system is crucial in overcoming obstacles. Surrounding yourself with the right people can provide encouragement, guidance, and accountability. Seek out individuals who share similar goals or have achieved what you aspire to achieve.

One way to find the right people is through networking events or professional organizations. Attend industry conferences or join online communities where you can connect with like-minded individuals. Seek out mentors who can provide guidance and share their experiences.

It is also important to communicate your goals and challenges with your support system. Share your progress, setbacks, and achievements with them. Their feedback and encouragement can help you stay motivated and provide valuable insights and advice.

Embracing Failure: Learning from Mistakes and Moving Forward

Failure is an inevitable part of overcoming obstacles. It is important to embrace failure as a learning opportunity rather than a setback. By reframing failure, you can extract valuable lessons and use them to improve and grow.

One way to embrace failure is by adopting a growth mindset. Instead of viewing failure as a reflection of your abilities or worth, see it as a chance to learn and improve. Embrace challenges and see them as opportunities for growth rather than obstacles to avoid.

Another way to embrace failure is by seeking feedback. Ask for constructive criticism from mentors, colleagues, or friends. Use their feedback to identify areas for improvement and make necessary adjustments to your approach.

Celebrating Success: Recognizing Achievements and Staying Motivated

Celebrating success is important in overcoming obstacles. It provides motivation, boosts confidence, and reinforces positive behaviors. Take the time to acknowledge and appreciate your achievements along the way.

One way to celebrate success is by setting milestones or checkpoints along your journey. When you reach these milestones, take the time to reflect on your progress and reward yourself for your hard work. This can be as simple as treating yourself to something you enjoy or taking a break to recharge.

Another way to celebrate success is by sharing your achievements with others. Share your progress on social media or with your support system. Their positive feedback and encouragement can further motivate you to continue overcoming obstacles.

Taking Action and Rising Above Obstacles to Achieve Your Goals

Overcoming obstacles is a crucial aspect of achieving success in both our personal and professional lives. By recognizing and addressing our obstacles head-on, setting realistic goals, developing a positive mindset, building resilience, creating a plan of action, cultivating discipline, seeking support, embracing failure, and celebrating success, we can rise above our obstacles and achieve our goals.

It is important to take action and apply these strategies in our daily lives. Start by identifying your obstacles and setting realistic goals. Develop a positive mindset and build resilience to overcome setbacks. Create a plan of action and cultivate discipline to stay focused and motivated. Seek support from the right people and embrace failure as a learning opportunity. Finally, celebrate your achievements along the way.

Remember, overcoming obstacles is not always easy, but with determination, perseverance, and the right strategies, you can overcome any challenge that comes your way. So take action today and rise above your obstacles to achieve your goals.

Chapter 14: From Caterpillar to Butterfly: My Journey of Personal Transformation

Personal transformation is a concept that has fascinated humans for centuries. It is the process of undergoing a profound change, much like a caterpillar transforming into a butterfly. This metamorphosis is a beautiful and awe-inspiring sight to behold, and it serves as a powerful metaphor for the transformative journey that we can embark on in our own lives.

Just as the caterpillar goes through a series of stages before emerging as a butterfly, personal transformation involves a process of growth, change, and self-discovery. It requires us to shed old beliefs, habits, and patterns that no longer serve us, and to embrace new ways of thinking, being, and living. It is a journey that can be challenging and uncomfortable at times, but ultimately leads to greater happiness, fulfillment, and a sense of purpose.

The Catalyst for Change: Understanding the Need for Personal Transformation

There are many reasons why people may feel the need for personal transformation. Perhaps they feel stuck in their current circumstances, unfulfilled in their relationships or careers, or simply unhappy with the way their life is going. They may have a deep longing for something more, but are unsure of how to achieve it.

The catalyst for change often comes from a place of discomfort or dissatisfaction. It is the recognition that something needs to change in order for us to live our best life. This recognition can be painful and unsettling, but it is also the first step towards personal transformation.

The Process of Transformation: From Caterpillar to Chrysalis

The process of personal transformation can be likened to the stages that a caterpillar goes through before it becomes a butterfly. The first stage is the egg, where the seed of transformation is planted. This is followed by the larva stage, where the caterpillar begins to grow and develop.

Next comes the pupa stage, where the caterpillar forms a chrysalis around itself. This is a period of intense transformation, where the caterpillar breaks down its old body and rebuilds itself into a butterfly. Finally, the butterfly emerges from the chrysalis, ready to spread its wings and take flight.

In our own lives, personal transformation involves a similar process of growth, change, and rebirth. We must first recognize the need for change and be willing to let go of old patterns and beliefs. This is followed by a period of self-reflection and self-discovery, where we explore our inner world and uncover our true desires and passions.

The Struggle Within: Overcoming Resistance and Embracing Change

While personal transformation can be a beautiful and rewarding journey, it is not without its challenges. One of the biggest obstacles we face when trying to transform ourselves is resistance. We may resist change because it is unfamiliar and uncomfortable, or because we fear the unknown.

Resistance can manifest in many ways, such as self-doubt, fear, or a reluctance to let go of old habits and beliefs. It can be difficult to break free from the familiar and step into the unknown, but it is necessary in order to grow and evolve.

Overcoming resistance requires courage, perseverance, and a willingness to face our fears head-on. It also requires a shift in mindset, from one of scarcity and limitation to one of abundance and possibility. By embracing change and letting go of resistance, we open ourselves up to new opportunities and experiences that can lead to personal growth and transformation.

The Journey of Self-Discovery: Exploring Your Inner World

A key aspect of personal transformation is the journey of self-discovery. This involves taking a deep dive into our inner world to better understand ourselves and our motivations. It requires us to ask ourselves important questions such as: What do I truly want? What are my values? What brings me joy and fulfillment?

Self-discovery can be a challenging and sometimes uncomfortable process, as it requires us to confront our fears, insecurities, and limiting beliefs. However, it is also a deeply rewarding journey that can lead to greater self-awareness, self-acceptance, and a sense of purpose.

There are many tools and practices that can support the journey of self-discovery, such as journaling, meditation, therapy, and self-reflection exercises. These practices can help us to uncover our true desires and passions, and to align our actions with our authentic selves.

The Power of Mindset: Harnessing the Power of Positive Thinking

One of the most powerful tools we have for personal transformation is our mindset. Our mindset is the lens through which we view the world, and it has a profound impact on our thoughts, emotions, and actions.

A positive mindset is essential for personal transformation, as it allows us to see challenges as opportunities for growth, and setbacks as stepping stones towards success. It helps us to cultivate resilience, optimism, and a belief in our own abilities.

Cultivating a positive mindset requires practice and intention. It involves reframing negative thoughts into positive ones, practicing gratitude, and surrounding ourselves with positive influences. By harnessing the power of positive thinking, we can transform our lives and create a more fulfilling and purposeful existence.

The Importance of Self-Care: Nurturing Your Mind, Body, and Spirit

Self-care is an essential component of personal transformation. It involves taking care of ourselves on all levels - mind, body, and spirit - in order to support our growth and well-being.

Self-care practices can include activities such as exercise, healthy eating, getting enough sleep, spending time in nature, practicing mindfulness or meditation, engaging in hobbies or creative pursuits, and nurturing our relationships.

Taking care of ourselves allows us to recharge our batteries, reduce stress, and cultivate a sense of balance and well-being. It also helps us to stay focused and committed to our personal transformation journey.

The Role of Gratitude: Cultivating a Grateful Heart for Personal Transformation

Gratitude is a powerful practice that can support personal transformation. It involves cultivating a grateful mindset and focusing on the positive aspects of our lives, even in the face of challenges or adversity.

Practicing gratitude has been shown to have numerous benefits, such as increased happiness, improved relationships, and better physical and mental health. It can also help us to shift our perspective and see the world through a lens of abundance and possibility.

There are many ways to cultivate a grateful mindset, such as keeping a gratitude journal, practicing mindfulness or meditation, or simply taking a few moments each day to reflect on the things we are grateful for. By cultivating gratitude, we can transform our lives and create a greater sense of joy, fulfillment, and contentment.

The Benefits of Personal Transformation: Living a Fulfilling and Purposeful Life

The benefits of personal transformation are vast and far-reaching. When we embark on the journey of personal transformation, we open ourselves up to new possibilities and experiences that can lead to greater happiness, fulfillment, and a sense of purpose.

Personal transformation allows us to break free from old patterns and beliefs that no longer serve us, and to create new ones that align with our true desires and passions. It helps us to uncover our unique gifts and talents, and to share them with the world in a meaningful way.

By transforming ourselves, we also have the power to transform the world around us. When we live authentically and in alignment with our values, we inspire others to do the same. We become beacons of light and hope, and we contribute to creating a more compassionate, loving, and harmonious world.

The Challenges of Transformation: Overcoming Obstacles and Staying the Course

While personal transformation is a beautiful and rewarding journey, it is not without its challenges. There will be times when we feel stuck, overwhelmed, or unsure of ourselves. We may face setbacks or obstacles that test our resolve and commitment.

During these times, it is important to remember why we embarked on the journey of personal transformation in the first place. We must stay focused on our goals and remind ourselves of the benefits that await us on the other side.

It can also be helpful to seek support from others who are on a similar journey or from a mentor or coach who can provide guidance and encouragement. Surrounding ourselves with positive influences and like-minded individuals can help us to stay motivated and committed to our personal transformation.

Embracing Your Transformation and Living Your Best Life

In conclusion, personal transformation is a powerful and transformative journey that can lead to greater happiness, fulfillment, and a sense of purpose. It requires us to let go of old patterns and beliefs, and to embrace new ways of thinking, being, and living.

While personal transformation can be challenging at times, it is also deeply rewarding. It allows us to uncover our true desires and passions, and to live authentically in alignment with our values. It empowers us to create a life that is meaningful, purposeful, and fulfilling.

So, I encourage you to embrace your personal transformation journey. Take the first step towards change, and trust in the process. Know that you have the power within you to create the life you desire. Embrace your transformation and live your best life.

Don't miss out!

Visit the website below and you can sign up to receive emails whenever Travis Breeding publishes a new book. There's no charge and no obligation.

https://books2read.com/r/B-A-CBXDB-DTFXC

BOOKS 2 READ

Connecting independent readers to independent writers.

Did you love *Rise: Mastering Confidence, Mindfulness, And Self-Esteem*? Then you should read *Celebrating Neurodiversity*[1] by Travis Breeding!

[2]

"Celebrating Neurodiversity" is not just a book; it's a manifesto for acceptance, understanding, and inclusivity. Breeding passionately advocates for the celebration of differences, urging readers to embrace the mosaic of neurodiversity that enriches our society. Through empowering stories of resilience, creativity, and innovation, Breeding showcases the immense potential that lies within the neurodivergent community.

From the unique ways in which neurodivergent individuals perceive the world to the invaluable insights they offer, "Celebrating Neurodiversity" is a thought-provoking exploration of what it truly

---

1. https://books2read.com/u/4DnjxP

2. https://books2read.com/u/4DnjxP

means to be neurodivergent. Breeding's empowering narrative inspires readers to challenge preconceived notions, foster empathy, and champion diversity in all its forms.

Whether you're a neurodivergent individual, a caregiver, or simply curious about the intricacies of the human mind, "Celebrating Neurodiversity" is a must-read that will leave a lasting impact. Join Travis Breeding on a journey of self-discovery, acceptance, and celebration as we embrace the kaleidoscope of neurodiversity and revel in the beauty of our differences.

Read more at breedingautismconsulting.com.

Also by Travis Breeding

Harmony in Flux: Navigating Bi-Polar Brilliance

The Friendship Rainbow

The Great Kindergarten Adventure: A Story about Going to School with Autism

The Magic Forest Adventure

Unlocking Brilliance: Navigating Autism and Applied Behavior Analysis Towards a Radiant Future

Decoding Love: Navigating Dating and Relationships on the Autism Spectrum

Echoes of a Late Diagnosis: Unveiling the Spectrum Within

From Theory to Practice: Implementing Effective Autism Interventions St

The Amazing Adventures of Aiden and His Asperger's Superpowers

The Magical Adventures of Lily and the Enchanted Forest

Unlocking Potential: A Journey Of Discovery Through ABA Therapy

Unlocking Potential: Navigating Employment for Neurodiverse Talent

Unlocking the Spectrum: A Journey through Applied Behavior Analysis from an Autistic Perspective

Unlocking The Spectrum: Navigating The Complexity Of Autism With Advanced Strategies And Insights

Beyond The Spectrum: Insights From Autistic Adults

Beyond The Stereotypes

Breaking Barriers: Navigating Autism With Therapeutic Insight

Celebrating Neurodiversity

Watch for more at breedingautismconsulting.com.

About the Author

Travis is the author of over 50 books about autism spectrum disorder. He travelst he country sharing the mission of making the world a better place for autistic individuals. In his spare time Travis enjoys writing, walking, and watching sports.

Read more at breedingautismconsulting.com.

9 798223 544043